THE MANUAL OF HARMONICS

*The Harmonics of Nicomachus
and the Pythagorean Tradition*

THE MANUAL
OF
HARMONICS

OF NICOMACHUS THE PYTHAGOREAN

Translation and Commentary

by Flora R. Levin

PHANES PRESS
1994

© 1994 by Flora R. Levin

98 97 96   5 4 3 2

Published by Phanes Press, PO Box 6114, Grand Rapids, MI 49516, USA.

Book design and production: David Fideler

Library of Congress Cataloging-in-Publication Data

Nicomachus, of Gerasa
    [Encheiridion harmonikês. English]
    The manual of harmonics of Nicomachus the Pythagorean /
translation and commentary by Flora R. Levin.
    p. cm.
    Includes bibliographical references and index.
    ISBN 0-933999-42-9 (alk. paper) — ISBN 0-933999-43-7 (pbk.: alk. paper)
    1. Nicomachus, of Gerasa—Criticism and interpretation. 2. Music,
Greek and Roman—History and criticism—Early works to 1800.
3. Music—Theory—To 500—Early works to 1800. 4. Pythagoras and
Pythagorean school—Early works to 1800. 5. Music—Acoustics and
physics—Early works to 1800.   I. Levin, Flora R. II. Title.
ML168.N53L413   1993
781—dc20
                                        93-36916
                                              CIP
                                           MN

To Sam

Contents

List of Figures 8

Texts and Abbreviations 9

Introduction 13

Chapter One 33

Chapter Two 37

Chapter Three 45

Chapter Four 61

Chapter Five 73

Chapter Six 83

Chapter Seven 99

Chapter Eight 107

Chapter Nine 125

Chapter Ten 141

Chapter Eleven 153

Chapter Twelve 173

Appendix: Excerpts from Nicomachus 187

Bibliography 199

Index 203

List of Figures

Figure 1: The Music of the Spheres 50

Figure 2: The Relation Between Distance and Pitch of the
Planetary Voices 51

Figure 3. A Simple Monochord 145

Figure 4. A Pipe Divided into Four Equal Lengths 148

Figure 5. The Greater Perfect System 164

Figure 6. Thrasyllus' Division of the Canon 166

Figure 7. Table of Intervals 183

Figure 8. The Three Genera 184

Figure 9. A Fifteen-stringed Monochord or Polychord 188

Texts and Abbreviations

Cherniss   Cherniss, H. *Plutarch's Moralia*, Loeb Classical Library, vol. XIII, part 1. Cambridge: Harvard University Press, 1976.

CQ   *Classical Quarterly.*

Da Rios   Da Rios, R. *Aristoxeni Elementa Harmonica.* Rome: Typis Publicae Officinae Polygraphicae, 1954.

De Falco   De Falco, V. [*Iamblichus*] *Theologumena Arithmeticae.* Leipzig: Teubner, 1922; addendis et corrigendis U. Klein. Leipzig: Teubner, 1955.

Deubner   Deubner, L. *Iamblichi De Vita Pythagorica Liber.* Leipzig: Teubner, 1937.

Düring (Ptolemy) Düring, I. *Die Harmonielehre des Klaudios Ptolemaios.* Göteborgs Högskolas Årsskrift 36 (1930), 1. Reprint. Hildesheim: Georg Olms, 1982.

Düring (Porphyry) Düring, I. *Porphyrius Kommentar zur Harmonielehre des Ptolemaios.* Göteborgs Högskolas Årsskrift 38 (1932), 2. Reprint. Hildesheim: Georg Olms, 1978.

Friedlein   Friedlein, G. *Anicii Manlii Torquatii Severini Boetii De Institutione Musica.* Leipzig: Teubner, 1867. Reprint. Frankfurt am Main: Minerva GmbH, 1966.

HSCP   *Harvard Studies in Classical Philology.*

Heath

Heath, Sir Thomas. *The Thirteen Books of Euclid's Elements*. 3 vols. Cambridge: Cambridge University Press, 1925. Reprint. New York: Dover, 1956.

Hiller

Hiller, E. *Theonis Smyrnaei Philosophi Platonici. Expositio Rerum Mathematicarum ad Legendum Platonem Utilium*. Leipzig: Teubner, 1878.

Hoche

Hoche, R. *Nicomachi Geraseni Pythagorei Introductionis Arithmeticae Libri II*. Leipzig: Teubner, 1866.

Jan

Jan, Karl von. *Musici scriptores graeci*. Leipzig: Teubner, 1895. Reprint. Hildesheim: Georg Olms, 1962.

Jonker

Jonker, G. H. *The Harmonics of Manuel Bryennius*. Groningen: Wolters-Noordhoff Publishing, 1970.

JHS

Journal of Hellenic Studies.

Nauck

Nauck, A. *Porphyrii Philosophi Platonici Opuscula Tria. Vita Pythagorae*: pp. 14–39. Leipzig: Teubner, 1860.

NOH

The New Oxford History of Music. Vol. 1, *Ancient and Oriental Music*. Edited by E. Wellesz. London: Oxford University Press, 1957.

Pistelli

Pistelli, H. *Iamblichi In Nicomachi Arithmeticam Introductionem Liber*. Leipzig: Teubner, 1894.

REG   *Revue des Études Grecques.*

SEG   *Supplementum Epigraphicum Graecum.* Edited by J. J. E. Hondius, A. G. Woodhead, and J. and L. Robert. Leiden: Brill, 1923.

Tannery   Tannery, P. *Quadrivium de Georges Pachymère. Biblioteca Apostolica Vaticana Studie Testi,* vol. 94, pp. 97–199. Revised by R. P. E. Stephanou. Città del Vaticano, 1940.

TAPA   *Transactions and Proceedings of the American Philological Association.*

Vors.   Diels, H. and Kranz, W. *Die Fragmente der Vorsokratiker.* 12th ed. Dublin/Zürich: Weidmann, 1966.

Wehrli   Wehrli, F. *Die Schule des Aristoteles: Texte und Kommentar.* Vol. 2, *Aristoxenus.* Basel/ Stuttgart: Benno Schwabe & Co., 1945.

Winnington-Ingram   Winnington-Ingram, R. P. *Aristidis Quintiliani De musica libri tres.* Leipzig: Teubner, 1963.

Introduction

Nicomachus of Gerasa: The Man and His Work

NICOMACHUS was a Syrian Greek who was supremely eminent in mathematics, Pythagorean philosophy, arithmology, and harmonics. He was born in Gerasa, the city of the Decapolis east of the Jordan River near Bostra where less than one hundred years or so before his birth Christianity was coming into being. It was here in "the region of the Gerasenes" not far from the Lake of Tiberias (Sea of Galilee) that Jesus is said to have cured the demoniac named "Legion" and sent the swine of unclean spirits into the waters of the sea.[1]

About Nicomachus' life his contemporaries and successors tell us very little. But if their words are few in number, they greatly illuminate the reputation of this key figure in the history of mathematics and the Pythagorean tradition. Nicomachus' very name was equated with mathematical skill by his younger contemporary, one of the keenest and most cultivated observers of the intellectual life of the second century C.E., Lucian of Samosata. To see, for example, Lucian's words: "Indeed, you do your computations just like Nicomachus of Gerasa!" is to understand what sort of position Nicomachus must have had in his day.[2] So great in fact was the conspicuousness of Nicomachus in mathematics that more than three centuries later he was still held in awe by the towering Neoplatonist, Proclus (410 or 412–85 C.E.). A very religious man, a visionary and, at the same time, a dialectician with a penchant for mysticism, Proclus saw himself as a link in the "Hermetic chain"—a series comprising those true philosophers who were destined to receive supernatural communications from Hermes.[3] What gave Proclus admittance into this illustrious company was revealed to him in a dream—one whose message he evidently accepted without question. The message was this: there was incarnate within him the soul of Nicomachus himself. With this endowment, Proclus was made eligible for inclusion among the greatest thinkers of all time. More conventional tributes to

Nicomachus' celebrity come from the great polymath, Porphyry of Tyre (232/3–c. 305 C.E.), who numbered Nicomachus among the most illustrious of the Pythagoreans and, as late as the seventh century C.E., from the encyclopedic scholar, Isidore, the Bishop of Seville, who placed Nicomachus' name on a par with that of the Master himself, Pythagoras of Samos.[4]

In his own day and for generations thereafter, Nicomachus seems to have been to arithmetic what Euclid was to geometry. Indeed, it was even said of Nicomachus: *Arithmeticam Samius Pythagoras invenit, Nicomachus scripsit* (Pythagoras of Samos invented arithmetic, Nicomachus composed it).[5] To be sure, Nicomachus was no Euclid when it came to scientific and inductive reasoning, and his deficiencies in this respect lead him into an occasional misconstrual.[6] This did not prevent his work from being highly esteemed, however; for whatever the limitations scholars may see in it today, it was appreciated in antiquity for the virtues it still exemplifies: orderliness, clarity, and conciseness. In it, Nicomachus makes no claims to originality of content; but he was original in his intent. For he designedly brought together for the first time centuries of Pythagorean arithmetic thought in language that everyone could understand. Not surprisingly, then, Nicomachus came to be regarded as the leading expert of the day in Pythagorean arithmetic theory and his work was in constant demand by the Greek intellectual community.

In time, the Romans must have registered an urgent appeal for it, and before the second century C.E. was ended, it was translated into Latin by one of the great luminaries of the Roman world: Apuleius of Madaura in Africa, the author of the *Metamorphoses*, better known as "The Golden Ass." We know that Apuleius was born of good family about 125 C.E. and while still a young man he journeyed to Alexandria, afterwards travelling through various African cities giving lectures on philosophy and religion. Latin was not his native language nor, it seems, was arithmetic his central interest. Apuleius' translation of Nicomachus' treatise into Latin was an intellectual feat, therefore, and it honored Nicomachus greatly. If Apuleius was engaged on this project around the middle of the century, it is possible that Nicomachus was still alive, living perhaps in Alexandria where Apuleius would have gone to consult him on points of technical detail.[7] Unfortunately, Apuleius' translation has not survived, but it may have lasted long enough to have served as the basis for the Latin version that has come down to us—that of Boethius.[8] In any case, with his authority and reputation as a mathematican thus guaranteed by the efforts of such contemporaries and successors as Apuleius and Boethius, Nicomachus' *Introduction to Arithmetic* was henceforth copied, admired, imitated, translated (into Arabic), epitomized, and analyzed from late antiquity down through the Middle Ages and well into the sixteenth century.

Nicomachus emerged from Gerasa, but it is quite certain that he did not make his brilliant career in a city that was so far removed from the leading centers of culture as was Gerasa. On the contrary, a young man of the cultivation and refinement that is so well displayed in the language of the *Manual of Harmonics* would most likely have been sent off for advanced study to Alexandria, the city which Euclid himself made famous for mathematics back in the fourth century B.C.E. Here, Nicomachus would have had the opportunity to study everything that was to be known about mathematics from the best teachers to be found anywhere in the world. That Nicomachus indeed had the best training possible is certified by his countryman and great admirer, Iamblichus of Chalcis in Coele Syria (c. 250–c. 325 C.E.) In his commentary to Nicomachus' treatise on arithmetic, Iamblichus says:

> We find that in his *Art of Arithmetic* Nicomachus has treated everything about this subject in accordance with the thought of Pythagoras. For this man is great in the sciences and had as his instructors on the subject those most expert in mathematics; apart from this, he transmitted the science of arithmetic with exactitude and in accordance with an admirable regularity and theory, offering a marvelous exposition of the scientific principles.[9]

Nicomachus' *Introduction to Arithmetic*,[10] the treatise which won him Iamblichus' high praise and instant fame as well,[11] is one of two works only that have reached us in its entirety. The other is his *Manual of Harmonics*, which is complete in one book.[12] In addition to these two works, Nicomachus is known to have written numerous other treatises. Two of these have survived in part. One, a major work in several volumes entitled *On Music*, is quite possibly the treatise from which the ten *Excerpta Nicomachi* were extracted;[13] these are provided here in translation in the Appendix, pp. 189–97. Portions of the other work, the *Theology of Arithmetic*, are preserved in an anonymous treatise of the same title.[14] Originally in two books, this work was an application of the first ten numbers to the origin and the attributes of the gods. It is perhaps to this work that Nicomachus refers in *Excerpt* 6 (p. 194) when he cites a text composed by him on the number seven.

Nicomachus was immersed in Pythagorean thought and, as his extant works exhibit, he was motivated by its two main aspects: mathematics and theology. The books now lost, which he is known to have written or, in some cases, thought to have written, must have been dictated also by the same Pythagorean ideal. For Nicomachus, certainly, it was a contemplative ideal which led not only to the creation of mathematics, but also to the development of a mathematically dominated religion. A work by Nicomachus on geometry, for example, to which he refers in his *Introduction to Arithmetic*,[15] would have been modelled no doubt on that of the great Pythagorean spokesman, Euclid.[16] Like Euclid's *Elements*, it would have started most likely with axioms which are supposedly self-evident and would have proceeded thence by deductive reasoning to arrive at theorems which are far from self-evident.[17] Above all, it would have made explicit the assumption on which all Pythagorean thought was grounded: geometry, with arithmetic, is an incontrovertible tool of the sister sciences, astronomy and harmonics.[18]

That being the case, any Pythagorean worthy of the name could ill afford to neglect those sciences which arithmetic and geometry so necessarily serve. Not surprisingly then, a lost treatise on astronomy is attributed to Nicomachus, one in which he was said to have discussed a Pythagorean hypothesis of eccentric circles.[19] Finally, a full-scale treatise on harmonics which Nicomachus mentions in the first chapter of his *Manual* as a projected work, was entitled, like his work on arithmetic, *Introduction*, and was presumably comparable to the *Introduction to Arithmetic* in its breadth and elaboration.

Taken together, these lost treatises, in addition to Nicomachus' extant work on arithmetic, would have constituted a whole course in the Quadrivium, or curriculum of the four mathematical sciences: arithmetic, geometry, astronomy and music or, as it was understood by the Pythagoreans, harmonics. For Nicomachus as for all other Pythagoreans, the study of music was completely mathematical in nature and was formalized as such in the curriculum of the Quadrivium. Thus, the four subjects—arithmetic, geometry, spherics (astronomy), and harmonics—were linked together by being described solely in terms of number. Accordingly, arithmetic was the study of number *per se* or absolute. And geometry, in recognition of its capacity to arrest the heavenly bodies in their courses at any given moment in paradigmatic figures, was construed to treat of quantity immobilized. Since geometry, in its deployment of points, lines, planes, and figures, all of which are governed by numerical cycles and quantities, depends on number, it and all it treats of cannot be disjoined from that science naturally prior to it: arithmetic. Astronomy, whose subject of inquiry is in effect quantity in motion, itself comprehends both geometry—the science of quantity at rest—and arithmetic—the science of numbers absolute and *per se*. It was, of course, Pythagoras who discovered the underlying factor which linked musical sound to number and made of it the science of applied arithmetic called harmonics. The momentous discovery which tradition associates with Pythagoras was this: the pitch of a sound from a plucked string depends on the length of the string, and the harmonious sounds that are given off by strings depend in turn on the ratio of those string lengths, these ratios being composed of simple whole numbers.

The exercise of mathematical reasoning and theological imagination must have enlarged the scope of Nicomachus' thinking considerably. We know from the remains of his arithmological treatise, for example, that he was induced to derive his theology from mathematics. It is conceivable then that the more straightforward mysticism of Asia which distinguishes Pythagorean thought from the intellectualized theology of Europe would in addition have led him to connect his astronomy, as did Ptolemy, with astrological beliefs.[20] While nothing can be stated for a certainty on this point, something lurking within the relics of evidence does raise the possibility. It concerns a mysterious and elliptical passage in Athenaeus[21] which associates Nicomachus with Egypt and cites him as an authority on a certain type of Persian drinking vessel that was apparently used by the Egyptians in'their libation ceremonies. Athenaeus derived his evidence on these ceremonies from what he identifies as the first book of a work by Nicomachus, entitled *On Egyptian Festivals*.[22] And Nicomachus' own source, according to Athenaeus, was a certain astrologer called Hermippus. If the Hermippus in question was the Syrian slave from Berytus (Beirut) who became a pupil of the learned authority on Phoenician religion, Philo of Byblos (64–141 C.E.), then he would not only be a contemporary and countryman of Nicomachus, but also a man with interests similar to those of Nicomachus. For, like Nicomachus, Hermippus is said to have written a work, presumably arithmological, on the number seven.[23]

Arithmology, as it was practiced by Nicomachus and the Pythagoreans, involved two kinds of mental activity: the mathematical and mystical insight. The leading proponent of the method in which these two kinds of mental activity were intimately combined was, of course, Plato. Understandably then, it was in Plato that Nicomachus was bound to find the logical development of the Pythagoreans' arithmological point of view. Indeed, throughout the Pythagorean tradition there persists a deeply embedded fusion of intellect and mysticism, but it is in Plato, above all, that mysticism finally gains the upper hand.

It is in the eighth book of Plato's *Republic*[24] in particular that mystical doctrines as to the relation of the human to the divine are reinforced by pure mathematics. The passage in question is, in fact, so recondite that it has spawned in its own right a history of interpretative writings that extends from Nicomachus himself down through the centuries into our own day. As yet, no one has solved the riddle of this *locus Platonis obscurissimus*, this most

obscure of all Platonic passages,[25] to the satisfaction of all the
scholars who have involved themselves in its explication. The one
person who might have shed light on this tantalizing Platonic
puzzle was Nicomachus. Regrettably, however, his discussion of
the passage is lost.

Nicomachus' discussion, to judge from what he says of it, was
contained in a *Commentary on Plato* which was quite possibly a
full-scale study of Plato's mathematical writings. The context in
which Nicomachus refers to his work on Plato concerns a mathematical curiosity: the fact that odd numbers multiplied by even
numbers always yield even numbers as their results:[26]

> In precisely the same way if an even number multiplies an even
> number, the product is always even and if odd multiplies odd
> always odd; but if odd multiplies even or even odd, the result will
> always be even and never odd. These matters will receive their
> proper elucidation in the *Commentary on Plato*, with reference to
> the passage on the so-called marriage [number] in the *Republic*
> introduced in the person of the Muses. So let us pass over to the
> third proportion, the so-called harmonic, and analyze it (trans.
> D'Ooge). [27]

Interestingly enough, in the passage from the *Republic* to which
Nicomachus refers, Plato never once uses the word *gamos* (marriage), nor does he speak of a marriage number. What he does say is
that there is a fundamental epitritic ratio of four to three which,
when joined to the number five and multiplied by three, produces
two harmonies or attunements (*harmoniai*). One of these, he says,
is the product of equal factors, while the other is the product of
factors of which some are equal and some unequal. As seems
evident then, Plato was dealing with the same sort of harmonic
mathematical formulae that Nicomachus had under discussion in
his *Introduction to Arithmetic*. And since these formulae exem-
plify the union or perfect attunement (*harmonia*) of opposites,
Nicomachus, in order to capture the basic idea underlying Plato's
elaborate geometric theorem, invented a metaphor by analogy in
which the four terms would be expressed as follows:[28]

a male and female (humans)
b marriage
c odd and even (numbers)
d multiplication

Accordingly,

$$a : b :: c : d$$

The metaphor is achieved when *b* is substituted for *d* (*d* for *b* also being potential), yielding "the marriage of numbers" (the multiplication of humans being also potential).

Nicomachus obviously took the *Republic* passage very seriously. What is more, he apparently understood it well enough to construe it metaphorically. Unfortunately, because he reserved his explanation for a more appropriate time, it is totally lost to us. But Nicomachus' metaphor seems to have been picked up thereafter by Iamblichus and later commentators, eventually becoming so widely disseminated that the Platonic passage has by now come to be designated variously as the Marriage Allegory, the Nuptial Figure, the Theorem of the Bride, etc., and the numbers resulting from this harmonic wedding of opposites as their "offspring," "progeny," and familial "generations."

Nothing, of course, was more influential on Nicomachus' sphere of thought than the teachings of Pythagoras himself. For it was in Pythagoreanism and its mathematical roots that Nicomachus, like Plato before him, found the chief source of his inspiration. Accordingly, Nicomachus learned everything he could about Pythagoras' mathematical interpretation of the universe; he also made himself an authority on Pythagoras' way of life. For, like all Pythagorean adherents, Nicomachus doubtless had in his beliefs a solid core of certainty which is fundamentally incommunicable except by a special way of life—a way of living which combines intellectual and moral discipline with wisdom. And wisdom, according to Nicomachus, was a term which Pythagoras restricted so as to apply solely to the knowledge of the truth—truth eternal and exact that inheres in the world of ideas as opposed to the world of illusory appearances. That being the case, anyone who lived in pursuit of this knowledge would be engaged in philosophy, for philosophy is, in Pythagoras' understanding of the word, the desire for and the pursuit of wisdom.[29]

The basis for Nicomachus' reputation as an authority on Pythagoras' life and thought was probably his *Life of Pythagoras*, now lost. Indeed, Porphyry in his own *Life of Pythagoras* cites Nicomachus as his primary source on Pythagoras' teachings and practices,[30] adding that Nicomachus' account of the Pythagorean friends, Damon and Phintias, for example, was based upon that of Aristoxenus' *Life of Pythagoras*.[31] And Iamblichus in his own *Life of Pythagoras* testifies to Nicomachus' authority on Pythagorean lore,[32] thus adding to the probability that there was extant before him a biography of Pythagoras written by Nicomachus himself.[33]

To be sure, marvellous stories about Pythagoras had been circulating for centuries long before Nicomachus—stories about Pythagoras' dominion over animals and mastery of their language, his mysticism and miracles, his portents and revelations, his control of space and time, and much more.[34] For Pythagoras, as these stories emphasize, was the possessor of divine wisdom, and all the ideas and concepts he inspired tended towards the otherworldly as against the false and illusory medium of the visible world. By Nicomachus' time, however, these stories had become an inextricable mixture of truth and falsehood. In setting himself to the task of sorting out the true from the false, Nicomachus, judging from the contents of his works, had a two-fold intent: first, to reveal Pythagoras as the originator of various Platonic doctrines;[35] second, to give final shape and definition to the life history of Pythagoras himself. It is Nicomachus' portrait of the man that is reflected in the later *Lives* of Diogenes Laertius, Porphyry, and Iamblichus.

In composing his portrait of Pythagoras, Nicomachus says that he was guided by sources both "ancient and trustworthy",[36] yet no one could have served as a greater inspiration to him than his remarkable older contemporary, Apollonius of Tyana. For Apollonius had not only written a biography of Pythagoras, he also modelled himself on Pythagoras, the man, even to the extent of

performing feats worthy of the Master himself. Indeed, that indi-
viduality which distinguished Pythagoras from all other mortals
was connected with his ability to triumph over space and time. As
Nicomachus reports it, Pythagoras was seen on the same day and
at the same time at Metapontum in Southern Italy where he was
later buried, and at Tauromenium in Sicily.[37] Amazingly enough,
such a feat was repeated by Apollonius, who was reportedly seen in
Smyrna and Ephesus on the same day. In any case, Apollonius,
quite apart from being a direct source for Nicomachus, would
understandably have been an especially suitable subject himself for
a biography by Nicomachus. As it happens, there is one piece of
evidence, unfortunately garbled, that has Nicomachus as the author of such a work—a *Life of Apollonius* of Tyana.[38]

Nicomachus lived, as we know, before the time of Apuleius,
whose translation of the *Introduction to Arithmetic* into Latin
provides a *terminus ante quem* for Nicomachus' lifetime. If we
assume that Apuleius had attained that degree of proficiency in
mathematics and Latin to permit his undertaking so formidable a
task, we might, given Apuleius' particular genius, place his translation sometime between 148 and 153 C.E., when Apuleius would
have been twenty-five to thirty years old. As for an earlier limit to
his lifetime, Nicomachus himself in the eleventh chapter of the
Manual gives us a positive *terminus post quem* with his reference
to Thrasyllus (died 36 C.E.), the personal astrologer to the Emperor
Tiberius.[39] Nicomachus lived, therefore, during the period between
the reign of Tiberius (died 37 C.E.) and the last years of Hadrian (died
138 C.E.) or the early years of Antoninus Pius, who was Emperor
from 138 to 161 C.E. That being the case, we can imagine Nicomachus
having been born about 60 C.E. and enjoying the years of his greatest
activity around the turn of the second century C.E. Trajan was now
Emperor and the world was peopled by such figures as Juvenal,
Plutarch, Theon, Epictetus and the great Ptolemy of Alexandria.[40]

Nicomachus was born in a land where Christianity had its
beginnings and he was growing up not too long after Saint Paul had
been making his way throughout the Near East and Greece,
gathering converts, setting up churches, and spreading the Gos-
pel.[41] If Nicomachus was very clearly untouched by any of these
developments, it was because he lived in a wholly different mi-

lieu—one in which it was not Christianity that was receiving the greatest encouragement, but Neopythagoreanism. Nicomachus' world was that of Alexandria where life and thought were dominated by Hellenistic culture, learning, and scholarship; where the *lingua franca* was Greek. It was the era of *Pax Romana* when scholars, merchants, and religious leaders seem to have been continually on the move. For travel had become, if not completely comfortable, then at least a little safer and more reliable for those who could afford it.

Of all Nicomachus' writings, it is only in his *Manual of Harmonics* that we learn something about the kind of man he was and the kind of life he was leading. For the situation he describes in the opening chapter most aptly mirrors the epoch in which he was living—one in which specialized Greek studies were enjoying their greatest impetus and scholars were commanding the highest esteem. It was a time when learned men like Nicomachus could, because of their expertise, find favor with someone of exalted rank—as Philostratus did, for example, with the Empress Julia Domna[42]—could enjoy enormous popularity and influence, could travel extensively, and could find numerous disciples and associates in diverse centers of culture.

Apart from the glimpses it gives of Nicomachus in action, the *Manual* has the special distinction of being the only work of its kind to reach us intact from the time of Euclid (c. 300 B.C.E.) to the second century C.E. Moreover, given the difficult conditions under which it was written, it must be considered as something of an intellectual feat. As Nicomachus tells us in the opening chapter, he was writing it while travelling, dictating it on the run to a scribe "after the manner of the ancients." Without benefit of leisure time for thought and reflection or his library for consultation, Nicomachus was not only composing the *Manual* in transit, but was also quoting by memory from the works of Philolaus (Chapter 9) and Plato (Chapter 8) and, without mentioning him by name, from Aristoxenus (Chapter 2 and Chapter 12). All these things considered, the *Manual*, despite its digressions and Pythagorean propagandizing, is a telling example of Nicomachus' talent for making a forbiddingly difficult subject intelligible to a non-specialist.

Notes to the Introduction

1. Matthew, 8.28–32; Mark, 5.1–13; Luke, 8.26–33. The area is called by various names: that of the Gerasenes (Luke), the Gadarenes (Matthew), the Gergesenes (King James).

2. The remark appears in Lucian's *Philopatris*, ch. 12.

3. See D'Ooge, pp. 77–78.

4. See D'Ooge, p. 78, n. 1.

5. Fabricius retrieved this phrase in the book entitled, *Altercatio synagogae et ecclesiae*, ch. I, for which see Ruelle (1881), p. 7.

6. See, for example, Heath (1921), I, pp. 98–99, who points out that Nicomachus seems to have been more interested in the mystic properties of numbers than in mathematical theory *per se*.

7. See D'Ooge, p. 124.

8. Nothing can be certain on this point. The greater probability is that Nicomachus himself was Boethius' primary source, the first three books of his *De institutione musica* based perhaps on Nicomachus' lost *Introduction*. For discussion, see Bower, pp. xxvi–xxvii.

9. *In Nicomachi Arithm.* (Pistelli, 4.12–16).

10. According to D'Ooge, p. 80, Iamblichus' title, *Art of Arithmetic*, is, in fact, a reference to Nicomachus' *Introduction to Arithmetic*.

11. As D'Ooge points out, p. 125, the greatest sign of Nicomachus' fame is the vast accumulation of commentaries on his *Introduction*. The latest of these to be published is that of *Asclepius of Tralles: Commentary to Nicomachus' Introduction to Arithmetic*, ed. by L. Tarán.

12. The ten extracts which appear in the *Appendix* are identified in some of the manuscripts as from the second book of the *Manual*. But these come undoubtedly from a different and longer work on harmonics, perhaps that to which Nicomachus refers several times in the *Manual*.

13. It was probably this longer work that was translated into the Arabic, in which it is entitled *Kitab al-musiqi al-kabir* or *Opus Maior de Musica*. See H. G. Farmer, "The Music of Islam," *NOH*, p. 458, 465.

14. See R. Waterfield, *The Theology of Arithmetic*, p. 23, who observes that "The treatise is, in fact, a compilation and reads like a student's written-up notes. Whole sections are taken from the *Theol-*

ogy of Arithmetic of the famous and influential mathematician and philosopher Nicomachus of Gerasa . . . At any rate, the treatise may tentatively be dated to the middle of the fourth century A.D."

15. *Introduction to Arithm.* 2.6.1 (Hoche, 83.3–4).

16. In Books 1–4 of Euclid's *Elements*, especially, the Pythagoreans are given their most penetrating interpretations. For discussion, see Michel, pp. 92–94. Not surprisingly, one ancient commentator was moved to say of Book IV that it "is the discovery of the Pythagoreans." See Heath (1921), I, p. 383.

17. On Euclid's deductive method, see Heath (1921), I, pp. 371–72.

18. This view is given explicit expression by Ptolemy, who says in the third book of his monumental treatise, *Harmonics* (Düring, 94.16–20), "Since both of these sciences use the incontrovertible instruments, arithmetic and geometry, for judging the quantitative and qualitative attributes of the primary motions, they are as first cousins, born of the sister senses, sight and hearing, and are reared as closely as possible by arithmetic and geometry."

19. The evidence for such a work is discussed by D'Ooge, p. 81. See also, note 22 below.

20. While the connection between astronomy and astrology is regarded by many today as incongruous, in antiquity and, certainly, in the middle ages no one seemed to consider it strange or perverse. Hence, Ptolemy's astrological work, *Tetrabiblos*, was accepted by the ancients as wholly consistent with his reputation as a scientific astronomer.

21. Athenaeus, 11.478A.

22. In treating of such festivals, Nicomachus had to have concerned himself with problems of the calendar and the ways in which the Egyptians regulated their festivals by phases of the moon. In other words, the driving force behind Nicomachus' study would have been astronomy, in particular the mathematical astronomy that provided a means of measuring time and fixing its passages. See Neugebauer, pp. 81–83.

23. On Hermippus, see *The Oxford Classical Dictionary*, 2nd ed., *sub nomine*.

24. Plato, *Rep.* 546A–D.

25. The passage is discussed and analyzed at great length by Brumbaugh, pp. 107ff. who also provides a history of its interpreta-

tions, pp. 143–50.

26. *Intro. Arithm.* 2.24.10–11 (Hoche, 131.2–12).

27. The word "number" is bracketed because it does not appear in the Greek text.

28. Metaphor by analogy is explained by Aristotle in his *Poetics* 21.6 as involving four terms such that the relation in which the second stands to the first is proportional to the relation in which the fourth stands to the third. The fourth term can therefore be substituted for the second, or the second for the fourth. As one example, Aristotle has old age is to life as evening is to day. Evening may therefore be called the old age of the day, and old age the evening of life, or "life's setting sun."

29. See the opening paragraph of Nicomachus' *Introduction to Arithmetic* 1.1; D'Ooge, p. 181.

30. Porphyry *Life of Pythagoras* 20 (Nauck, 21.22).

31. Porphyry *Life of Pythagoras* 59–60 (Nauck, 38.18–39).

32. Iamblichus *Life of Pythagoras* 35.251 (Deubner, 135.9–11).

33. According to Burkert, p. 98, we have direct access to Nicomachus' biography of Pythagoras, sections of which are in Nicomachus' original wording, through Iamblichus.

34. On Pythagoras as a superhuman figure, see Burkert, pp. 137ff.

35. See Levin (1975), pp. 49–50.

36. This statement comes to us by way of Iamblichus' *Life of Pythagoras* 60 (Deubner 32.23–24). Cf. Burkert, p. 141, n. 116.

37. See Burkert, p. 141.

38. Von Jan, p. 234, accepts the fact that Nicomachus wrote such a work, but D'Ooge, p. 81, finds the evidence to be too problematic to be taken as certain.

39. In addition to being the court astrologer to Tiberius, Thrasyllus was also celebrated for his writings on music. That he was a direct source for Theon has been demonstrated by D'Ooge, p. 42. See also, Levin (1975), pp. 9–10. The passages from Thrasyllus which were quoted by Theon have been translated by Barker (1989), II, pp. 211–13.

40. Nicomachus refers to Ptolemy in *Excerpt* 4 (p. 193), but scholars have argued that this reference does not constitute direct evidence that Nicomachus was familiar with the *Harmonics* of Ptolemy inasmuch as the reference may have been interpolated by a scribe or

commentator. Cf. Levin (1975), p. 10. n. 16. See Ch. 11 below, pp. 158–59.

41. Saint Paul and Saint Peter were executed c. 67 C.E., thus within a few years after Nicomachus' birth.

42. The biographer, Philostratus, was patronized by the Emperor Septimius Severus and his wife Julia Domna. He not only mingled with the luminaries of the imperial circle, but also traveled with the Empress and her entourage. It was at the Empress' behest that Philostratus undertook to write his *Life of Apollonius*. See Bowersock, *Greek Sophists in the Roman Empire*, pp. 4–5.

The Manual of Harmonics

by

Nicomachus of Gerasa

Chapter-headings of *The Manual of Harmonics*

by Nicomachus of Gerasa, the Pythagorean

1. The book is a manual outlining the doctrine of harmonics

2. On the two species of the voice, the intervallar and the continuous, and their regions.

3. Among objects of perception, the music of the planets is considered to be the prototype of our music according as we imitate it.

4. The properties in musical notes are regulated by number

5. Pythagoras, by adding the eighth string to the seven-stringed lyre, instituted the attunement of the octave

6. How the numerical proportions of the notes were discovered

7. On the division of the octave in the diatonic genus

8. Explanation of the references to harmonics in the *Timaeus*

9. The evidence of Philolaus

10. On the tuning of notes by means of numerical proportions

11. On the double octave in the diatonic genus

12. On the progression and division of the notes in the three genera

Manual of Harmonics

by Nicomachus of Gerasa, the Pythagorean
dictated extempore in the
manner of the ancients

Chapter 1

The book is a manual outlining
the doctrine of harmonics

EVEN though the study of intervals and their relations within
the harmonic elements is in itself complex and hard to encompass in a single commentary, and even though I, being otherwise in
a state of acute mental distraction because of the confusion and
haste occasioned by travel, am unable to devote myself to your
instruction on these subjects with the appropriate lucidity that
demands above all one's leisurely and undivided attention—nevertheless I must exert myself with all zeal, since it is you who bid me,
Your Noble Majesty, to set before you the main points in brief,
undocumented though they may be, without proper foundation
and detailed explication; so that, using this brief note as a manual,
you may, with one glance at the chapter headings, recall what is
discussed and explained at greater length in each chapter.

And if the gods are willing, as soon as I shall have leisure time and
a rest from my journey, I shall compose a longer and more detailed
Introduction for you on these same subjects, one that will be
thoroughly articulated and crammed, so to speak, with close
reasoning, and comprising several volumes. And at my first opportunity, I shall send it to you, wherever I hear that you and your
family are residing. In order that it be easier for you to follow, I shall
begin at roughly the same point as that at which I started your
instruction when I was explaining the subject to you.

Commentary 1

THE IDENTITY of the noble woman at whose request Nicomachus composed the *Manual* is, and promises to remain, a total mystery. That the lady in question was of exalted rank there can be no doubt, for Nicomachus' terms of address befit in every respect only a royal personage. Indeed, the lady could quite possibly have been a princess of one of Rome's Mesopotamian provinces; or, if she were Roman and proficient in the Greek language, as educated Romans were from the time of Horace onward,[1] she could even have been the consort of the Imperator himself. If, therefore, Nicomachus did not presume to address the lady by name, it was probably, in view of her rank, because titles alone were considered by him the most appropriate forms of address: *Ariste* and *Semnotate*, "Most Noble" and "Most August,"[2] or, as a Roman would say if addressing the Empress, *Optima* and *Augusta*. With this in mind, I have given Nicomachus' words the modern locution, "Your Noble Majesty."[3]

Whether Nicomachus' correspondent was Greek or Roman cannot, of course, be known, but one thing is certain: Nicomachus responded with alacrity to her request for instruction in harmonics and treated it with the utmost seriousness. To be sure, her station in life would have demanded nothing less. Still, Nicomachus' esteem for the lady seems to have been as much for her intellectual powers as for her commanding rank. For, as is obvious from his language, Nicomachus thought her to be everything that is superlative: *philokalotate*,[4] "most cultivated," *hemerotaton*, "most patrician," and *noemonestaton*, "most intelligent."[5]

From all indications then, Nicomachus' relations with his noble correspondent were not unlike those of Hadrian with his imperial patroness, Pompeia Plotina, Trajan's Empress. It was of Plotina that Hadrian once said accordingly, "Though she asked much of me, she was never refused anything."[6] That being the case, Nicomachus did as Hadrian would have done were he presented with a request, however inconvenient or ill-timed, from Plotina: he complied at once. Nicomachus therefore undertook to compose the *Manual* under most adverse conditions—those imposed by travel. It is quite likely that he was travelling by sea, yearning, as he apparently did, for land where his mind would be serene or, as he put it, *akymanto*, "without waves." As matters stood, however, he was suffering turmoil and dislocation, having only his own knowledge to consult and a scribe to write down his words as he pronounced them. His words were dictated, as he says, *ex tempore*, by which he meant "from memory," since there were no treatises at his disposal such as the great library at Alexandria would have provided him.

From the glimpse, however slight, that Nicomachus gives us of his professional activities, he seems to have been living the life of one of the regular sophists of the Empire, journeying from one major intellectual center to another in the Roman world, lecturing on Pythagorean mathematics and philosophy to appreciative audiences, teaching selected students, and settling only temporarily at some designated sophistic center like Smyrna or Tarsus.[7] Among his students was the addressee of the *Manual*, an obviously avid learner with whom Nicomachus had met on any number of former occasions for the purpose of her instruction, offering her, most likely, vital information on those subjects prerequisite to the study of harmonics—arithmetic and metrical geometry or, as it was then understood, geometry of the straight line.[8]

While he was waiting to learn the current address of his correspondent—for the lady, too, was in transit with her entourage[9]—Nicomachus engaged himself in the composition of this technical *Manual*. Although he deprecated it for the brevity of its treatment, we may suppose that it satisfied his noble patroness for the clarity of its exposition and the various kinds of problems that it brought to her attention. As we read the *Manual*, then, we can envisage its author at sea, well-accomodated, as would befit a man of his stature, on a strong and roomy Alexandrian vessel. In addition to passengers like Nicomachus, his ship may have been carrying a cargo of Egyptian wheat, linens, delicate pottery and phials of precious Egyptian balsams to various ports in Phoenicia and Syria Palestrina—to Sidon, or Tyre, or to Caesarea. On the completion of the *Manual*, Nicomachus would quite possibly have set foot in one of these ports, staying long enough to learn of the noble lady's whereabouts, there to dispatch his anxiously awaited treatise.

Notes to Chapter 1

1. Horace, *Carmina* 3.8.5.
2. Jan, 236.17.
3. On Nicomachus' terms of address, see W. C. McDermott, "Plotina Augusta and Nicomachus of Gerasa." Compare Levin, *Nicomachus*, p. 17.
4. Jan, 242.14.
5. Jan, 265.3–4.
6. See McDermott, above, n. 3, 197–98.
7. On the cities and activities of sophists under the Empire, see Bowersock, *Greek Sophists*, pp. 18–19.
8. The science of canonics, which was invented by the Pythagoreans, is in all of its essentials applied metrical geometry. According to its procedures, each musical pitch is represented by a length on the canon or rule, a length that is practically measurable. For, given any magnitude on the rule, it is possible to discover what the number is to which that magnitude has a relation. It is to this sort of procedure that Nicomachus refers at the end of Chapter 11 in his critique of Eratosthenes and Thrasyllus and their divisions of the canon. Compare Levin, *Euclid*, 430–31.
9. Jan, 238.11–12.

Chapter 2

On the two species of the voice, the intervallar and the continuous, and their regions

THE ADHERENTS of the Pythagorean school maintained that there are two species of the human voice subsumed under one genus; they called them the continuous and the intervallar, specifically, deriving their names from the attributes of each. The intervallar, which is the species of melody, stops on every note and renders the change in all the parts perceptible, they assumed to be free from confusion, discrete and graduated by the magnitudes of the intervals lying between each note, forming a progressive series, as it were, and not a blending of the parts of the voice lying adjacent to one another, these being well-defined, readily distinguished and in no instance dissolving into one another. For the melodic species is such that, to trained ears, it renders clear all the notes and the size of the interval in which each note participates. If, on that account, one were to deviate from this species of the voice, he would be said no longer to be singing but to be speaking. The other species is the continuous whereby we converse with one another and read, there being no need for us to make the pitches of the notes explicit and discrete from one another as we string together our discourse right up to the completion of our utterance. For if a person, whether in conversation or in recounting some event or in reading aloud, makes manifest the sizes of the intervals between each note by spacing and changing his voice from one note to another, such a one is said to be speaking or reading no longer, but to be singing. Now since the human voice has two parts, they thought it reasonable that there also be two regions which each of these parts passes through and occupies; that the region of the continuous species is by nature indeterminate in its compass, assuming its own limit from whatever point the speaker begins until he stops, that is, from the first utterance to the final silence, so that it is regulated for the most part by us.

The region of the intervallar species, however, is no longer subject to our control, but to that of nature, and is itself limited by different operations. For its beginning is the first sound that can be perceived by the ear, while its final limit is the utmost sound that can be uttered by the voice. Our awareness and discrimination of the compasses of notes and their changes relative to one another begin at the point at which our sense of hearing receives its very first stimulus, it being possible that fainter sounds not yet perceptible to us are also produced in nature though they still elude our ears. As an example, in the case of weights, there are certain bodies which are almost impossible to express in terms of weight—chaff or bran or other such things; but when such items are added together and the balance-beam of the scale begins to move down, then we say that the first quantum of scientifically determined weight takes place. So too, when the faintness of the voice is intensified little by little to a greater point, we calculate the first degree that is perceptible to our ears to be the beginning of the region of the singing voice. However, it is not our sense of hearing that determines the end of the region, but the human voice. For we define the final limit of the region of this type of voice at that point which it reaches in its melodic progress as it advances musically.

Let it make no difference to us for the present whether we discuss the human voice or that of stringed, wind, and percussion instruments constructed in imitation of our voice; rather, let us pass over for the present the difference between them so that we do not dissipate our explanation at the very outset.

Commentary 2

THE GENUS under which the two species of the human voice are subsumed is motion (*kinesis*), the continuous motion being that of the speaking voice, the intervallar being that of the singing voice.[1] These species of vocal motion and the region or *topos* in which they transpire involve a concept of motion that is prodigiously abstract and, above all, wholly unnatural for anyone who works, as did Nicomachus, with the ordinary material of mathematics. It is a concept that exists inside the framework of Aristotelian thought, wherein number, weight, and measure carry no philosophical significance.[2] In short, it is a concept of motion with which mathematics can have no concern simply because the motion in question is not strictly locomotive and does not transpire in observable physical space. Rather, the motion in question is a process of change that is directed toward a verbal or, as the case may be, a melodic end. And, as any observant Aristotelian would maintain, there is no mention of verbal or melodic ends in mathematics.

The motion of which Nicomachus speaks has a rich and multiple content equivalent to what an Aristotelian would view as a universal becoming. As such, it belongs to a universe whose space is a qualitative *continuum*, so to speak, where each pitch has a proper melodic place and function, and where the place of each corresponds to the full realization of that function. Within this *topos*, or *continuum*, there are only two directions in which the voice can move: up and down;[3] but there are countless ways in which the voice can effect changes of quality and aspect. To an Aristotelian, all these changes are "motions." At the same time, the *topos* in which these motions transpire is defined in Aristotelian terms solely by the things that move within it. Accordingly, Aristotle would construe the *topos* as that which contains the thing that moves—the thing, in this case, being the human voice—the *topos* being a *continuum* which is neither greater nor less than the things it contains, but one that is fully occupied by what it contains.[4]

Applied to the phenomena of music, this strictly Aristotelian concept of *topos* would hold that the *topos* in which the human voice moves is defined on the one hand by what the moving voice is capable of doing, and on the other, by what the human ear can apprehend the moving voice to be doing.[5] It was on the basis of this Aristotelian concept of motion as a dynamic process, and *topos* as a qualitative *continuum*, that Aristoxenus of Tarentum (born *c.* 360 B.C.E.)—Aristotle's pupil at the Lyceum and the leading musical theorist of antiquity—formulated his uniquely Aristotelian theory of music. Not surprisingly then, Aristoxenus opened his *Harmonic Elements* with the subject: vocal motion, the better to distinguish song from speech. For, as Aristoxenus realized, song had to be the focus of any theory of music. Accordingly, Aristoxenus discriminated between the two motions of the voice—the continuous motion of speech and the intervallar or discrete motion of song—within the *continuum* or *topos* in which they both move. In so doing, he had every right to assert, as he does, that he, Aristoxenus, was the first writer on music ever to have described these species of vocal motion in their proper terms:

> In both of these motions there is, clearly, a high and a low—indeed this motion, and the high and the low toward which the voice moves, occurs in space (*topos*)—but the species of each movement is not the same. Yet no one has ever carefully defined the difference between each of these motions before this writer.[6]

By the time Nicomachus undertook to compose the *Manual*, the ancient writings on music had long been dominated by the principles of vocal motion and melodic space which Aristoxenus had enunciated for the first time in his *Harmonic Elements*. For theorists attempting thereafter to give a scientific account of music's harmonic properties, the established convention was to begin, as Aristoxenus did, by distinguishing song from speech on the basis of the motion of the voice involved in each kind of activity. Thus Nicomachus, like many a theorist before and after him, adhered to this convention in the opening of this second chapter of his *Manual*. But he went far beyond the dictates of this Aristoxenian construction by crediting it entirely, and most improperly, to the Pythagoreans. Indeed, not only did he ignore Aristoxenus' prior claim to this sort of analysis, but, by attributing this concept of motion to the followers of Pythagoras, contravened the entire Pythagorean approach to harmonic science. For simply put, motion and space meant one thing to an Aristoxenian, but quite another to a Pythagorean. Motion, on the Aristoxenian construal, is the fulfilling in melody of what exists potentially in the voice; while space is the vertical *continuum* that is delimited by and is coincident with the melodic elements it contains.[7] And this construal is wholly incompatible with Pythagorean thought. For motion was construed by the Pythagoreans as the physical, observable, and measurable cause of sound; while space was viewed by them as an absolute dimension subject solely to the laws of mathematics.

To a Pythagorean, as Nicomachus is at pains to demonstrate in the *Manual*, melodic space is purely mathematical, its dimensions absolute, fixed, and unchangeable. Within this absolute space there is a place for each note of the scale and, because each of these places is fixed by the laws of mathematics, it must be the true location of any pitch. This location, which is ordained for any pitch by mathematical law, is therefore the pitch's absolute place. Taken in the aggregate, these absolute places for pitch form the coordinates of the Pythagorean-Platonic universe. This universe, as Plato demonstrated in the *Timaeus*, extends over four octaves and a major sixth and comprises one genus only—the diatonic.[8] Thus, by dealing, as does Nicomachus in the *Manual*, with the spatial distances between pitches as absolute mathematical certainties, their collective truths uncontaminated by sensory experience, the Pythagoreans could prove that melodic space is irrational—that whole-tones are indivisible mathematically, that semi-tones and all the other micro-intervals which were employed by ancient Greek musicians, such as quarter-tones and thirds of tones, are only auditory chimeras.[9]

As Nicomachus must have known, the mathematics of the Pythagoreans had one object: the uniform and permanent universe of the quantitative; while the musical metaphysics of the Aristoxenians had quite another: the manifold and infinitely varied domain of the qualitative. Nonetheless, he misapplied one method—that of Aristoxenus—to something that was never its specific object—number. His purpose seems clear, however: to promote, in whatever way he could, the primacy of Pythagoras and the Pythagoreans in all things harmonic.[10]

Notes to Chapter 2

1. The ancient theorists' aim in distinguishing between speech and song was to reach a formal definition of a musical note (*phthongos*), the smallest indivisible element in auditory sensation. See Chapter 12, p. 173 (Jan 261.4). This procedure differs fundamentally from that of modern theorists who usually begin their treatises on acoustics by defining musical sound as distinguished from noise. See the opening of Chapter 4, p. 61 (Jan 242.20–243. 2). The convention is discussed by Johnson, 51. For the ancient Greeks, drawing a clear distinction between speech and song was a matter of special difficulty because of the inherent musicality of the spoken tongue with its built-in pitch accent. For a full examination of this phenomenon, see Stanford, pp. 27ff.

2. What did have philosophical significance for Aristotle was how the universe and everything in it worked so as to achieve its perfected form. To pursue this line of thought, Aristotle appealed not to number, but rather to the concepts: *dynamis*, how things *can work*; *energeia*, what they do when they *are working*; and the final form they take when their *work is completed*. This meant studying things having a separate, substantial existence and how they change or move from potentiality to activity and to completed form. As Aristotle saw it, mathematics, and, hence, number, could deal only with things that are devoid of movement and have no separate existence. Thus, a mathematician must study things in abstraction from the whole fact of change or motion. See Ross (1936), pp. 26–36. Cf. Cherniss (1935), pp. 385–86.

3. Aristotle's terms in *Physics* 211a5, "up" and "down" (ἄνω καὶ κάτω) belong to the world of vision; they correspond to Nicomachus' "treble" and "bass" (ὀξύς καὶ βαρύς), terms that represent the ear's perception of "high" and "low." The *topos* in question here is what Aristotle *Physics* 212b5 characterizes as a *continuum* (συνεχές) that is, by definition, homogeneous (ὁμοιομερές).

4. Aristotle, *Physics* 211a1–7.

5. These are the sole criteria by which Aristoxenus ascertained the maximum compass and the minimal internal intervals of the musical *topos*. They are, as is evident, strictly non-mathematical. See

43

Aristoxenus, *Harm. El.* 1.14 (Da Rios 19.5–16).

6. Aristoxenus, *Harm. El.* 1.3 (Da Rios, 7.13–18).

7. "Vertical" is a term borrowed from the world of vision that corresponds with the tonal *continuum* along which the ear locates the elements of melody. "Vertical" denotes the sort of illusion experienced by all people, an illusion which does not correspond to the physical object to which it refers—a vertical plane, for example—but one which represents, nonetheless, a genuine perception of the musically cognitive ear.

8. To construct his cosmic scale, Plato (*Timaeus* 36A2–B5) began with a series of terms—1, 2, 3, 4, 8, 9, 27 (a combination of the two geometric progressions—1, 2, 4, 8, and 1, 3, 9, 27)—between the terms of which he inserted the harmonic and arithmetic means. See Levin (1975), pp. 89–91; Brumbaugh, pp. 227–28. See below, Chapter 8, pp. 114ff.

9. The problem was that however vast the implication mathematical harmonics had for related sciences such as astronomy and acoustical physics, its dictates were singularly restrictive for musicians. For however much the harmonicians and technicians wrangled and disputed over proper tunings and measurements of strings, they could agree on one thing only: the distribution of the diatonic octave. For some, this was sufficient since it was grounded, as Plato had shown, in mathematical logic, the five whole-tones of the diatonic scale evenly distributed over the space of an octave. The two *leimmata* or "left-over" semi-tones expressible in the ungainly ratio 256:243 were approximated by modern acousticians to 19:18. For Nicomachus' version of this distribution, see Chapter 8. To musicians, however, this distribution must have been altogether unsatisfactory. The reason for this was that in the actual practice of music, performers were negotiating intervals smaller than such semi-tones, intervals like the *diesis* (quarter-tone), *eklysis* (a flatting by three quarter-tones), *ekbole* (a rise of five quarter-tones), and *spondeiasmos* (a rise of three quarter-tones).

10. See Levin (1975), pp. 46ff.

Chapter 3

Among objects of perception, the music of the planets is considered to be the prototype of our music according as we imitate it

IT IS probable that the names of the notes were derived from the seven stars which traverse the heavens and travel around the earth. For they say that all swiftly whirling bodies necessarily produce sounds when something gives way to them and is very easily vibrated; and that these sounds differ from one another in magnitude and in region of the voice either because of the weights of the bodies or their particular speeds, or because of the position in which the motion of each is accomplished, these positions being more subject to fluctuation or, conversely, more resistant. These three differences are clearly observed in the case of the planets, which differ from one another in size and speed and position as they whir continuously and without pause through the ethereal expanse. Hence the word ἀστήρ (star) was formed, inasmuch as each is deprived of στάσις (status quo) and is ἀεὶ θέων (constantly running), whereby the words θεός (god) and αἰθήρ (ether) were also formed. However, from the fact that the movement of Kronos is the farthest up from us, the lowest pitched note in the octave was called *hypate*, for *hypaton* means the highest up. On the other hand, from the fact that the course of the Moon is the lowest of all and is situated nearer to the earth, the name *neate* was derived, for *neaton* signifies the lowest. The term *parhypate* was derived from the position of Zeus, being below Kronos on one side, while at the other side, the position of Aphrodite, being above the Moon, occasioned the name, *paraneate*. The term *mese* was derived from the Sun's most central position, this being the fourth from either end, since the *mese* in fact stood at a distance of a fourth in the ancient heptachord. The term *hypermese*, also called *lichanos*, was derived from one of the positions on either side of the Sun, that of Ares, which was assigned the sphere between Zeus and the Sun. On the other side of the Sun between Aphrodite and the Sun, the position occupied by Hermes provided the name *paramese*.

We shall provide more detailed substantiation respecting these identifications, complete with linear and numerical examples, in the commentaries we promised you earlier, Your Most Serene Highness, and we shall explain why we ourselves do not hear this cosmic symphony with its deep complementation of sound and its all-embracing attunement, as tradition describes. But now, because of the pressure of time, we must run over the material that follows.

Commentary 3

NICOMACHUS' purpose in the second chapter of the *Manual* was to define the essential property of a musical note—music's smallest indivisible element.[1] This was stated by him to be an unwavering pitch upon which the voice stations itself in the intervallar species of motion. But the question as to exactly *where* the voice is to station itself so as to produce the discrete pitches of melody is for the laws of mathematics to determine, as Nicomachus will explain in Chapter 4. In the present chapter, his ostensible purpose is to demonstrate that the musical notes were named after and, hence reflect, the positions or *epochai*[2] of the seven planets relative to Earth. With Earth taken to be the unmoving center of the universe, the following "planets" are explained by Nicomachus to orbit the earth in their allotted *epochai* (calculating from the most distant one—Kronos—to the nearest—the Moon):

Planet	Name of Note	Pitch
Kronos	hypate	E
Zeus	parhypate	F
Ares	lichanos or hypermese	G
Sun	mese	A
Hermes	paramese or trite	B♭
Aphrodite	paranete	C
Moon	nete	D

This series of notes yields the fundamental form of attunement (*harmonia*)—the heptachord—according to which the ancient musical scales or *systemata* were constructed.[3] It is an attunement of two diatonic tetrachords, each comprising the intervals: semitone, whole-tone, whole-tone, and both joined together on the common note A or mese. The resulting scale structure covers a total range of a minor seventh or one whole-tone less than an octave:

E   F   G   A   B♭   C   D

According to Nicomachus, the names given to these notes designate the pitch positions in the scale that correspond (in the most literal sense) to their planetary counterparts in the heavens: hypate (highest), parhypate (next to the highest), hypermese (above the mese), the term used by Nicomachus to denote lichanos (finger-note), mese (middle), paramese (next to the middle), the term used by Nicomachus to denote trite, the third note descending of the conjunct tetrachord, paranete (next to the lowest), and nete (the lowest).

As if to assure his learned reader that his derivation of these terms was neither capricious nor idiosyncratic, Nicomachus reminds her of other words whose etymological roots had also been located among the heavenly phenomena by no less an authority than Plato himself. The name Plato did not have to be mentioned as the author of these etymologies, however, for Nicomachus took it for granted that his correspondent had read the *Cratylus*. There Plato related ether (αἰθήρ) to "ever on the run" (ἀεὶ θέων); and he claimed that the heavenly bodies were called "gods" (θεοί) because they, too, are always "on the move" (θέω). On the other hand, the word "star" (ἀστήρ) was connected by Plato, doubtless for its brilliance, to "lightning" (ἀστραπή).[4]

Supported by such etymological precedents, Nicomachus could not but persuade his reader of the authenticity of his derivations. In truth, however, these derivations appear to be Nicomachus' own inventions. For one thing, they are not to be found anywhere else in the literature; for another, the names of the musical notes are commonly held to be reflective not of the planets' positions in the heavens, but rather, of the strings' positions on the lyre.[5] According as the lyre was held by the performer, the strings were thus in the positions highest or "hypate" in relation to the hand, and lowest or "nete" in relation to the hand. With "mese" being the string in the middle of the group of seven, "lichanos" then fell within the reach of the "forefinger," after which it was named. Taken in terms of the voice's pitch range, however, the pitch of the string in the highest position or "hypate" turns out to be the lowest in the scale (E); while "nete," the string in the lowest position, produces the highest pitch in the scale (D). Only "mese," the name of the "middle" string, coincides in meaning with the pitch that occupies the middle position among the seven notes of the scale.

In framing his cosmic etymologies for the names of these notes, Nicomachus' intention was not simply to explain the musical nomenclature. On the contrary, he had a much more fundamental purpose in raising this etymological issue, namely, to focus the attention of his reader upon the principle that gave rise to the whole complex mathematical, harmonic, and cosmic doctrine of the Pythagoreans. For miraculously enough, the dialectical steps by which the Pythagoreans proceeded to convert music—the most unfathomable of the arts—into a branch of mathematics, were diverted by them, as Nicomachus testifies, to transform astronomy—the most conspicuous and mathematical of the sciences—into the unheard archetype of music. Their point of departure was, as Nicomachus is at pains to show in this chapter, motion (kinesis). Accordingly, he explains, if motion is the cause of sound, and the primary exemplar of motion is present in the whirlings of the celestial bodies through space, it should follow that these macrocosmic motions of the planets must themselves produce sound.[6] Moreover, that the sounds presumed thus to be generated are musical pitches may be attributable to the continuous, uniform, and regular motions that the planets execute in their orbits. And since the relative pitch of any musical sound is a function of the velocity of the moving object, the pitches emitted by the planets coursing through the ether should necessarily vary in accordance with their individual speeds. The variation in pitch imputed to the planets is thus explained by Nicomachus to be a function of their mass, speed, and orbital position.

With this line of reasoning, the conditions were set for so thorough a union of harmonics and astronomy that henceforth the mathematical laws underlying the one could be held to account for the harmonic perfection perceived in the other. There was required only the addition of a single proposition that would complete an incorruptible circle of necessity wherein harmonics and astronomy would find their common bond in number: that the harmonic sectioning of the heavens by the planets moving in their allotted regions must be presumed to have yielded a consonantal distribu-

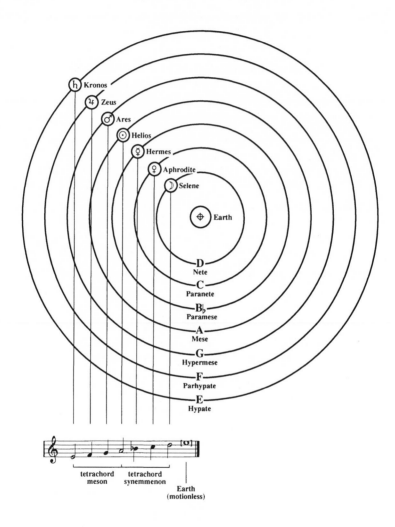

Figure 1. The Music of the Spheres according to *The Manual of Harmonics*, Chapter 3.

tion of pitches corresponding to that of a well-attuned musical scale. What Nicomachus is in fact suggesting in this chapter is, therefore, that the intrinsic symmetry manifest in the heavens must be echoed in the imperceptible, but harmonically propertied

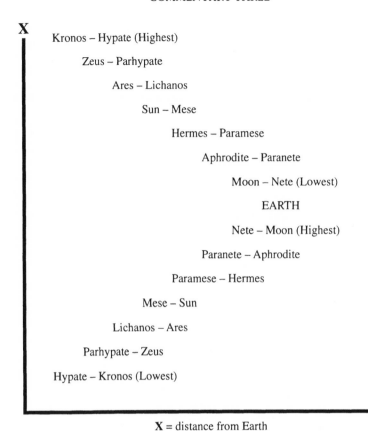

X

Kronos – Hypate (Highest)

Zeus – Parhypate

Ares – Lichanos

Sun – Mese

Hermes – Paramese

Aphrodite – Paranete

Moon – Nete (Lowest)

EARTH

Nete – Moon (Highest)

Paranete – Aphrodite

Paramese – Hermes

Mese – Sun

Lichanos – Ares

Parhypate – Zeus

Hypate – Kronos (Lowest)

Y

X = distance from Earth
Y = pitch line

**Figure 2. The Relationship between Distance and Pitch of the
Planetary Voices.**

voices of the heavenly spheres.[7] And on this basis, the evidence of
numerical relations provided by the musical elements could sys-
tematically be used as axioms to account for the distribution of the
planets in the heavens. Thus, by virtue of their being distant from
one another in the same relative degrees as the notes of a well-
attuned musical scale—these degrees of difference dictated by the
mathematical ratios determining the consonantal intervals em-

bodied in the octave—the planets could be shown to trace harmonic boundaries in the heavens. And, conversely, the structural elements of music could be said to imitate the heavenly paradigm in all of its particulars.

The task of reconciling this conception of a harmonic universe with the astronomical phenomena produced diverse theories and rationalizations assembled under the traditional title, "Harmony of the Spheres."[8] In this chapter, Nicomachus provides what may be the most ancient version of this distinctly Pythagorean-Platonic concept. He begins, as did Plato, by enlisting only those propositions whose truth can be established by mathematics. From that point on, he saw to it that his concept of celestial motion should rest upon the same mathematical bases as those underlying acoustical motion. In this respect, he followed the Pythagoreans and Plato in lifting what appears to be a romantic caprice into the precincts of science. The result is that his version of the harmonious universe as well as those of others—in particular, that of Plato in the *Timaeus*—were henceforth to influence astronomical thought for centuries, eventually to converge with cosmic reality in the celestial physics of Kepler.[9]

Little is known for certain about the original form of the doctrine of planetary music, since neither Pythagoras nor his immediate successors left any written account of it. No trace of it is to be found in the extant fragments of Philolaus, the first Pythagorean to leave any writings at all.[10] The first allusion to the doctrine appears in the *Republic* where Socrates refers to the Pythagorean view that "astronomy and harmonics are sisters."[11] But it is in the myth of Er that Plato provides the first detailed account of the "Harmony of the Spheres."[12] According to Plato, eight sirens are seated on eight whorls of the spindle of necessity, each one representing, respectively, the sphere of the fixed stars, Sun, Moon, and the five planets. Each siren sings one note only, these corresponding *in toto* to the sequence of notes in a musical scale consisting of eight notes or an octachord. In Plato's version, the highest pitched note, or nete, is assigned to the circle of fixed stars, while the lowest note, hypate, is assigned to the Moon; in other words, we get an arrangement that is the reverse of Nicomachus' assignments, or:[13]

Sphere	Name of Note	Pitch
Fixed Stars	nete	E¹
Kronos	paranete	D
Zeus	trite	C
Ares	paramese	B
Hermes	mese	A
Aphrodite	lichanos	G
Sun	parhypate	F
Moon	hypate	E

As Nicomachus had explained it, the differences in the pitches of his scale depend upon the size, speed, and position of the moving bodies. Although he does not establish the principle relating speed of movement and pitch until Chapter 4, where he states that pitch varies directly with speed, this principle quite obviously applies in his assignments of pitch to the heavenly bodies.[14] On the dictates of this principle, the highest-pitched note must therefore be produced by the swiftest-moving body, and the lowest-pitched note by the slowest-moving body. That being the case, Kronos, on Nicomachus' conception being situated farthest from the earth, or hypate, must be the slowest-moving planet and for that reason must produce the lowest-pitched note. And the Moon, situated lowest in the heavens or nearest to the earth, must be the swiftest-moving body, producing therefore a note of the highest pitch, or nete. According to Nicomachus' system, then, the sounds emitted by the seven moving celestial bodies correspond to the seven notes of a heptachord, the most primitive form of the scale up to the time of Terpander (fl. mid-seventh century B.C.E.).[15] And the highest pitches in this scale are assigned by him to the swiftest-moving bodies, while the lowest pitches are given to the slowest-moving bodies.

Such a system, in which the body closest to the earth—the Moon—emits the highest sound, while that farthest from the earth—Kronos—emits the lowest sound, is based upon the independent orbital revolutions of the planets around a stationary Earth. That Earth is stationary in Nicomachus' system can be assumed from the fact that no note is assigned to it. For if the Earth were in motion, it would produce a sound, and hence be assigned a pitch. In other words, Nicomachus' system is a geocentric one in which the distances of the planets is calculated from Earth as the center of the universe.

Both these notions—geocentricity and independent movement of the planets—most likely go back to Pythagoras himself. Indeed, there seems to be little doubt that Pythagoras regarded the universe as spherical, enclosing the earth in the middle, and rotating about an axis passing through the center of the Earth. The key to the movement of the whole heavenly sphere about the earth as center is *time*. Accordingly, the heavenly sphere, or sphere of fixed stars,[16] was conceived by Pythagoras as revolving from east to west about an axis passing through the center of the earth in a period of twenty-four hours. Its revolution was thus diurnal. The assumption of this diurnal revolution of the sphere of fixed stars further suggests the immobility of the earth.[17]

Pythagoras is credited also with having made the important distinction between the diurnal revolution of the sphere of fixed stars from east to west and the independent movement of the planets in an opposite direction.[18] This discovery accounted for the impression of variation in the movement of the planets, an impression induced by their absolute speeds as they were carried in the diurnal revolution of the heavens from east to west and their relative speeds as they each accomplished their independent orbits from west to east around the earth. Thus, the planets closest to the outer sphere of fixed stars appear to move *swiftest* in a period of twenty-four hours, this being their *absolute* speed; while their independent movements describe in the same period of time only a portion of their orbits and thus appear to move *more slowly* as they are closer to the outer sphere of fixed stars, this being their *relative* speed.[19] In accordance with these views, the planets, regarded in terms of their diurnal movements, appear to move swiftest as they are farthest from the earth and consequently would be assigned the highest pitches in the scale of sounds; viewed in terms of their independent orbital movements, however, they appear to move slowest as they are farthest from the earth and would on this basis be assigned the lowest pitches. Thus, their order in respect to their absolute speed—that is, their speed in the diurnal revolution of the heavens from east to west—is the reverse of their order in respect to their relative speed, that is, their independent orbital movements from west to east.

Judging from the fact that Nicomachus assigned the highest pitch to the body lying closest to the earth—the Moon—and the lowest pitch to the body lying farthest from the earth—Kronos—his criterion for these assignments must have been the independent revolutions of the planets in their orbits, his order determined in respect to their relative speeds. Thus, the Moon, which describes its orbit the fastest (in about a lunar month), is assigned nete, the highest pitch; while Kronos, which describes its orbit the slowest (in about thirty years), is assigned hypate, the lowest pitch. It is, therefore, the time-period in which the orbital movements of the planets are accomplished that is the critical factor in Nicomachus' system. The speeds of the moving bodies, calculated in a twenty-four hour period, are thus seen to be slowest as they are farthest from the earth, and fastest as they are closest to the earth.

Interestingly enough, in *Excerpt 3*, (p. 192), Nicomachus tells us of another version of the harmony of the universe, one which he alleges to antedate his own.[20] In this system, the musical pitches are assigned to the planets in a reverse order, this order being based upon the older theory that all the heavenly bodies revolved in the same direction from east to west. Accordingly, Kronos, being nearest to the outer sphere, would be considered as moving the fastest in twenty-four hours, while the Moon, being innermost, would move the slowest. On this basis, the pitch of Kronos would be the highest, while that of the Moon would be the lowest.

All things considered, however, the system recorded by Nicomachus in the *Manual* incorporates two notions which do stem from a high antiquity and which may in fact go back to Pythagoras himself. These two notions are: geocentricity and the independent movements of the planets. To be sure, traces of later influences are present in Nicomachus' account, which may be summarized briefly. First, the names of the gods were scarcely usual for the planets in the time of Pythagoras. With the exception of the Sun and the Moon, the planets were designated by adjectival epithets. Kronos was *Phainon,* "the shining one," Zeus was *Phaethon,* "the brilliant one," Ares was *Pyroeis,* "the fiery one," Aphrodite was *Phosphoros,* "the light bearer," and Hermes was *Stilbon,* "the gleaming one." The earliest instance in Greek literature of the use of a god's name for a planet (Hermes) appears in the *Timaeus* of Plato.[21]

Second, and equally anachronistic, is the fact that in Nicomachus' system the Sun occupies a middle position in the order of planets counting from the Moon to Kronos. This middle position of the Sun was not asserted until the Alexandrian period. In the order of planets generally recognized by the Pythagorean astronomers of the fifth century B.C.E., by Plato in the *Timaeus,* and by Eratosthenes, the Sun was fixed after the Moon, so that in the oldest system, the order was: Moon, Sun, Aphrodite, Hermes, Ares, Zeus, Kronos.[22] Only in Alexandrian times did the realization come that the Sun must be fixed beyond Aphrodite and Hermes. The respective positions of Hermes and Aphrodite seem, however, to have been unsettled in antiquity and this is reflected in Nicomachus' ordering where Aphrodite is followed by Hermes in the *Manual,* but is reversed in *Excerpt* 3.[23]

As mentioned earlier (p. 47), Nicomachus' ordering of the cosmic scale is based on the ancient heptachord, a conjunctive scale-structure that is associated with the name of Terpander. Formed by the conjunction of two tetrachords of the same intervallic distribution, this scale covers a total range of a minor seventh. But oddly enough, in identifying hypate, the pitch of Kronos, Nicomachus calls it the lowest note "in the octave" (*to dia pason*),[24] despite the fact that his scale falls short of the octave by a whole-tone. Moreover, according to his testimony in Chapter 5, the octave resulted from Pythagoras' having added an eighth string to the heptachord. Whatever the reason for the discrepancy, it seems minor enough in the light of the larger issue, namely, that of the harmonious universe.[25] And this, as Nicomachus is concerned to explain, was established on the basis of the number seven, a number which seems always to have provoked a search for correspondences: the seven ages of man, the seven vowels of the Greek alphabet, the seven days of the week, etc.[26] Above all, then, parallels established between the seven planets and the heptachordal scale were based on the distinctly Pythagorean view that the whole universe and everything in it was in a perfect attunement or *harmonia* over which number ruled supreme.

Notes to Chapter 3

1. See Chapter 12, p. 173; Jan 261.4–5.

2. On the meaning of *epochai* as "orbital positions," see Levin (1975), pp. 35–37. Cf. Barker, II (1989), p. 251, n. 17.

3. The Greeks' notion of pitch in the formation of scales was not, as ours, that of a comparison with an external standard; rather, they framed abstract models of scales and based their transcriptions on the relations obtaining between the pitches of those scales. The method whereby musicologists translate the Greek scales and pitch relations into modern notation is based on an equivalence between our A_2 and the sign C of Greek notation, which corresponds to the note, mese, of the Hypolydian key. On this whole question, see Chailley (1979), pp. 76–77; 103–04. The convention used here for indicating musical pitches is that of Carl E. Seashore, *Psychology of Music* (New York, 1967), p. 73.

4. Plato's etymologies appear in *Cratylus* 410B, 397D, and 409B, respectively. His etymology of ether was adopted by Aristotle in *De Caelo* 270b24.

5. In other words, the Greeks did not, as some scholars have conjectured, call high pitches "low" and vice versa. See Henderson (1957), p. 345.

6. According to Aristotle, *De Caelo* 290b–291a, the Pythagoreans believed that the planets produced musical notes whose pitches were determined by their velocities and that their velocities were in turn determined by their distances; their distances from one another, moreover, were in the same ratios as the consonant intervals within the octave. For additional references, see Levin (1975), p. 2, n. 2.

7. The question as to why we on earth do not hear these voices was examined by Aristotle, *De Caelo* 290b34–35, who suggests that if the moving planets did produce sounds as a result of their motion, these sounds would be so massive that they would cause widespread destruction on Earth. Others have suggested that we are so accustomed to the sounds of the planets that we no longer actually hear them. See R. Bragard (1929), 207–08. Elsewhere, Nicomachus says (Iamblichus *De Vita Pyth.* 66 [Deubner, 37.2ff.]) that only a superior being such as Pythagoras has the power to hear the heavenly music.

8. The epochal discovery which ancient authorities attribute to Pythagoras, that musical pitches depend on numerical proportions and that the underlying principle of *harmonia* is a numerical system bound together by interlocking ratios, quite possibly led to the idea of the harmony of the spheres. For here it could be shown that the laws of the macrocosm, the heavens, are discoverable by analogy with those that govern the microcosm, the elements of music on Earth. For discussion, see Heath (1913), pp. 46–47; Philip (1966), pp. 123–28.

9. The truth of universal harmony was finally given incontrovertible expression when Johannes Kepler discovered the laws of planetary motion: that the planets trace elliptical orbits; that the squares of the period of revolution of any two planets are in the same ratio as the cubes of their mean distances from the sun; that one focus of each planetary ellipse is occupied by the sun. See Merleau-Ponty and Morando (1982), pp. 148–51.

10. Although the Greek doxographers ascribed an elaborate cosmological system to Philolaus, Aristotle never mentions his name in connection with it, but gives it as the theory of the "so-called Pythagoreans" or of "some Pythagoreans" (*De Caelo* 293a18–293b30). Cf. Heath (1913), p. 48.

11. Plato, *Rep.* 530D.

12. Plato, *Rep.* 617A–B.

13. See Heath (1913), pp. 152–57.

14. Jan, 243.9–10.

15. On the seven-stringed lyre which Terpander inherited from his predecessors, see *Excerpt* 1, p. 189; Jan 266. The extension of the heptachord to an octachord is credited to Terpander by some sources, as, e.g., Ps.-Aristotle, *Problems* 19.23, and Ps.-Plutarch, *De mus.* 1140F. In Chapter 5, Nicomachus offers the counter-testimony that Pythagoras was responsible for the addition of the eighth string.

16. The term "fixed" (*aplanes*) was given to those stars grouped into the stable configurations or constellations which appear to the unaided eye as permanently fixed on the celestial sphere. These stars, because they revolve as a unit, as though fastened to a solid, outer sphere, give the impression to the naked eye of an overwhelming permanence. The uniformity and regularity of the diurnal motion of this fixed sphere provided a model of uniform time and its perceived

kinship with number. For discussion, see Merleau-Ponty and Morando (1982), pp. 14–17.

17. See Heath (1913), pp. 49–50.

18. Theon of Smyrna (Hiller, 150.12–18) thus states categorically that Pythagoras was the first to notice that "the planets move according to a regulated revolution, simple and equal, but from which results, *by chance,* an apparently varied and irregular motion" (tr. by R. and D. Lawlor, p. 98).

19. On this distinction between absolute and relative velocity of the planets, see Heath (1913), pp. 107–08.

20. Jan, 272.9–12.

21. *Tim.* 38D2. The names of all the planets appear for the first time in Plato, *Epinomis* 986E3–987C7. See Tarán (1975), pp. 300–01.

22. See Plato, *Tim.* 38D1–3.

23. Jan, 272.3–5.

24. Jan, 241.19–20.

25. In Chapter 5, Nicomachus explains that the conjunction of two tetrachords of the same form must result in a range one whole-tone less than an octave. It is probable that the discrepancy resulted from his desire to make Pythagoras the undisputed inventor of the octachord. Cf. Barker, II (1989), p. 252, n. 23.

26. See *Excerpt* 6, p. 194; Jan 276.8–278. 9. Cf. commentary to Chapter 5, p. 74. It should be noted that Nicomachus' use of the uncontracted forms *neate* and *paraneate* reflects an ancient Pythagorean tradition. On these forms, see below, pp. 129–30.

Chapter 4

The properties in musical notes are regulated by number

WE SAY that sound in general is a percussion of air that is unbroken in its progress to the ear; a note, however, is a pitch without breadth of a melodic voice, and that pitch is a kind of persistence and a sameness of a note that is without intervals in its extent. An interval is a kind of passage from low to high or the reverse. A system is a synthesis of more than one interval.

When a considerable blow or breath falls upon the surrounding air and strikes it in many parts, a loud sound is produced; when a small blow or breath falls upon the surrounding air, a soft sound is produced; when a regular blow falls, a smooth sound is produced; when an irregular blow falls, a harsh sound results; when the blow is applied slowly, a low sound is produced; when quickly, a high sound results.

Wind instruments, such as auloi, trumpets, panpipes and hydraulic organs, necessarily have inverse properties and the same things hold true for the stringed instruments, such as the cithara, lyre, spadix and similar instruments. There are instruments that appear to be intermediate between these in the sense that they share common properties and are subject to the same affects; these are the monochords, commonly called pandouroi but which the Pythagoreans call canons. Classed also among the stringed instruments are the triangular harps; and there are also the transverse auloi along with the photinxes, as the coming discourse will show.

Among stringed instruments, the greater and more powerful the tension, the greater and higher pitched are the notes produced; while the lesser tensions produce more slow moving and lower pitched notes. For when the plectrum displaces the strings, some, when shifted from their proper position, return very quickly and with considerable vibration, striking the surrounding air many times, as if impelled by the very intensity of the tension; on the other hand, others return to their position along the instrument maker's plumbline slowly and without vibration.

Again, in wind instruments the greater bores and greater lengths produce a slow moving and relaxed note. For if the breath, extenuated by a long air-column, issues forth into the surrounding air and strikes and agitates it without much force, the resulting note is low pitched.

We must observe here that the greater and the lesser depend upon the quantity we obtain by our own tightening or slackening of strings, or by our own lengthening or shortening of the parts of air-columns. Wherefore, it is abundantly clear that all these factors are governed by number. For quantity is held to be the property of number and number alone.

Commentary 4

ANYTHING that can be weighed, measured, or counted is representable by number. For quantity, whether it be predicated of weight, of size, or of speed, is the property of number and number alone. That being the case, Nicomachus sees it as his task in this chapter to isolate for his student those factors in the production of sound that are in fact measurable and can thus be represented by number. He begins by explaining how it was possible for the Pythagoreans to represent a single pitch by a number, an interval comprising two pitches by a numerical ratio, and a musical scale or synthesis of more than one interval by a complex of more than one ratio. In achieving this scientific goal, the Pythagoreans, animated by the discoveries of Pythagoras himself, succeeded in translating what the ear alone can apprehend into the concrete numerical terms that the mind can contemplate. In so doing, they made accessible to the intellect the mathematical laws that govern the production of music's objective phenomena—pitch and interval.

The two factors in sound production that the Pythagoreans found to be subject to mathematical law, as Nicomachus explains, are speed of vibration in the air and the size of the sound-producing body. The first of these factors—speed of vibration—was alluded to briefly in Chapter III, where Nicomachus spoke of the medium through which the planets unceasingly whirl. There he characterized this medium as something that is easily vibrated, literally, "set into waves" (kymainomenos).[1] Here, he speaks of air as being percussed and thereby set into a motion that is unimpeded or unbroken in its progress to the ear. This ongoing motion in the air induced by a percussion of some sort came routinely to be defined by the Pythagoreans as sound.

In arriving at this definition of sound, some of the ancients laid stress primarily on the percussion itself, as did, for example, Archytas of Tarentum (early fourth century B.C.E.), who said:

> There cannot be a sound without there first being a blow of one thing on another.[2]

Others, like Adrastus (middle of the second century C.E.), a Platonic and Aristotelian scholar, focussed essentially on the medium that is percussed, as, he says, did the Pythagoreans who preceded him:

> He [Adrastus] says that the Pythagoreans dealt systematically with these matters: since every melody and every note is a type of melodic utterance, and every melodic utterance is a sound, and sound is a percussion of air that is prevented from being dissipated, it is clear that if the air remained stationary, there would be neither sound nor melodic utterance, in which event there would be no musical note.[3]

Like Nicomachus, Adrastus thereupon referred variations in the pitch and loudness of musical notes to the speed and vehemence of the vibrations in the air:

> When there is a blow, and a movement in the air occurs, if the movement is swift, a high note is produced; if slow, a low note; if vehement, a loud sound is produced; if gentle, a soft sound.[4]

Interestingly enough, however, it was Aristotle, the critic par excellence of the Pythagoreans, who provided for them the very definition of sound they were seeking:

> Air is implicated in hearing . . . Air itself is soundless because of its being easily dispersed. But when it is prevented from being dispersed, its very motion is sound.[5]

Aristotle's point was that air is the medium through which sound is transmitted, but it is not the agent that initiates the sound. The initiator of sound, he says, is a percussion that sets an object into vibration, and this vibration is in turn communicated to the surrounding air or water (Aristotle realized that water, like air, is a conductor of sound).[6] Aristotle, and Plato as well, were both astute enough to make a distinction, therefore, between the object struck and the stroke made by the air in motion on the ear. This stroke or percussion made by the vibrating air upon the ear is what accounts for the sensation of hearing or, as Plato put it:

> We may therefore define sound in general as a blow given by the
> air through the ears to the brain and the blood and transmitted to
> the soul.[7]

As is evident from these various accounts, the ancients understood that three systems working in close collaboration were
required for the production of sound in general and of musical pitch
in particular. The first system is a sounding instrument; the
second, a medium that transmits the sound; the third, the ear that
receives the sound. They understood also that what links these
systems together is a certain type of motion, one which is propa-
gated from the sounding instrument to the ear in the form of
ongoing waves to which the ear is sensitive. Accordingly, as
Aristotle so well described it in the *De Anima*, it is an instrument
which emits sound, a medium which transmits it, and the ear
which registers it. As Nicomachus explains, therefore, all the
different varieties of sound that the ear detects can be referred to the
type of motion that is induced in the air and to the primary source
of this excitation of the air. Moreover, like Adrastus, he explains,
with great assurance, that it is the speed of this motion that
determines the pitch of a musical note. To illustrate this point, he
enlists musical instruments of various types and, in the process,
provides historical information of more than passing interest for
instrumentalists and organologists.

Despite the certainty with which Nicomachus presents the facts
respecting vibration as a quantitative factor in the production of
pitch, both he and the Pythagorean harmonicians who came before
and after him were faced with a fundamental difficulty: they had no
method for measuring the rate of vibration that was involved in
pitch production. And in consequence, they had no reliable method
of assigning to those vibrations the correct numerical values. To be
sure, Euclid in the Introduction to his *Sectio Canonis* (Division of
the Canon) showed himself to have been aware of the components
of vibratory motion and the role that they played in the production
of musical pitch. Indeed, he even invented the proper technical

terms to describe their behavior: *pyknoterai* (condensations) and
araioterai (rarefactions). On the basis of these components, he
could assert that musical pitch is susceptible of being analyzed into
discrete parts, or *moria*,[8] each one being a function of the lateral
displacement of a string from its initial position. That being the
case, any increase or decrease of these components results in a
corresponding rising or lowering of the pitch produced. He rea-
soned, therefore,[9] that since all things composed of parts can be
spoken of in terms of the numerical proportions obtaining between
them, musical pitch, since it conforms so precisely in its variations
to the enumerative vibratory motion that causes it, ought to admit
of a similarly mathematical characterization. At the time of his
writing, however, he, like Nicomachus after him, had no way of
assigning to it the correct numerical values.

Theoretically speaking, the vibrations of a long string might have
been slow enough for Euclid or Nicomachus to count by eye; as a
practical matter, however, those of a short string would have been
far too fast for their eyes, or anyone else's, to calculate. Without a
scientific method for counting the wave-like parts of a vibrating
current in the air (a method that would be discovered only in the
distant future by Marin Mersenne, 1588–1648), and with no oscil-
loscope to render those parts visible on a fluorescent screen,
Nicomachus was at the same disadvantage as would be an astronomer working without a telescope.[10] Appeal to direct experience was
not possible. However, the Pythagoreans had transmitted to him a
useful hypothesis, one dictated by the facts of vibration, even
though it had to be extended beyond their warrant. Its truth is given
by Nicomachus in this chapter, and it consists in this principle: the
vibrational frequency of a stretched string is inversely proportional
to its length. This meant that the motion responsible for musical
pitch is in fact subject to laws of a mathematical nature.

To demonstrate how the principle of inverse proportion works,
Nicomachus examines the properties of three types of musical
instrument: winds, strings, and what he classifies as intermediate
instruments. As he explains, these instruments, no matter how
much they may differ in structure, all share the same properties: an
inverse proportion between the size of their sounding bodies and

the speed with which these bodies vibrate. Thus, the greater the dimension of the sounding bodies, the less is their speed of vibration; and conversely, the smaller the dimension, the greater is the speed of vibration. That this principle is borne out by the reciprocity between numerical ratios and fractions is explained by Nicomachus in Chapter 10. There he shows that the higher pitch is greater in the sense that it is represented by a number that is the reciprocal of the fraction that represents the size of the sounding body. In other words, the fractions representing string lengths, for example, have only to be inverted to account for speed of vibration in numerical terms. On this basis, greater with respect to string length (or length of air column) produces a lower pitch, while greater with respect to the reciprocal factor—vibration—produces a higher pitch.

This relation, which remains constant between dimension, vibration, and pitch, is manifest in all the musical instruments mentioned by Nicomachus.[11] To begin with, the winds—aulos, salpinx (trumpet), syrinx (panpipe), hydraulic organ—all share a common feature: vertical pipe construction. But they differ from one another in respect to the modes by which the air in their pipes was activated. Thus, the aulos was activated either by a double reed, like the modern oboe, English horn, or bassoon, or by a single reed, like the modern clarinet and saxophone. The syrinx or panpipe was set into vibratory motion by edge-tones whereby the breath is broken against an angular surface communicating with the air-column. This is what distinguishes the modern flute and piccolo from the other wood-winds. In the salpinx or trumpet, periodic impulses are produced in the air-column by the pressure of the lips against a mouthpiece, as is the case with the modern trumpet, cornet, bugle, French horn, trombone, and tuba. The hydraulic organ was essentially a large many-piped (*polykalamos*) syrinx, whose pipes of graduated size were set into vibration by the action of pumps, water pressure, and compressed air. It was said to have been invented by one Ctesibus of Alexandria, the son of a barber, sometime during the third century B.C.E.

The lyre, whose mythological history is given by Nicomachus in *Excerpt* 1,[12] is of the same construction as the cithara, which is essentially a larger and more heavily built lyre. Both instruments are composed of a frame and a resonating chest over which strings of equal length but different thicknesses and tensions are vertically strung. Each string when plucked by the finger or a plectrum vibrates in its total length and produces a single pitch. A set of tuning pegs, or *kollopes*, was used to alter the tension on each of the strings at a time, thus raising or lowering the pitch as need be. Both the lyre and the cithara were always associated with the lyricism, virtuosity, and musical inventiveness of antiquity's greatest composers and performers. That being the case, Nicomachus's introduction of the spadix into the company of these two instruments is perhaps the most curious occurrence in all of his writings. For the spadix, even from the little that we know of it, was obviously considered an instrument of ill-repute. Indeed, like other multi-stringed and high-pitched instruments, e.g. the sambuka, the spadix was associated with debauchery and licentiousness. As such, it was scrupulously debarred from the hands of all proper young ladies.

In illustrating lyre-type instruments, Nicomachus could just as easily have referred his reader to the more respectable barbiton or phorminx, both of them instruments of esteemed bards. That he chose to mention the spadix instead does, however, teach us something: the spadix was in its construction a lyre-type instrument.[13] Moreover, it must have resembled a "spadix," or palm-frond, the item after which it was named. Given its reputation, it was presumably *polychordia*, or multiple-stringed, a deplorable attribute according to the testimony of Quintilian.[14] What is worse, its strings must have been short, this guaranteeing that its voice was high and effeminate. In short, the spadix carried all the insignia of decadence and moral corruption. We cannot know why Nicomachus offered it for his noble reader's consideration; but we can hope that she did not hold it against him.

Instruments considered by Nicomachus to be intermediate among the strings are the trigonon, or triangular harp, and the examples of lute-type instruments: the pandoura, used strictly for musical purposes, and the monochords and canons, instruments used for acoustical research. Nicomachus distinguishes both these classes—

harps and lutes—from the lyre-type instruments, on the basis of their distinctive structural characteristics. Thus, whereas the strings of lyre-type instruments are strung parallel to one another and set at an equal distance from the sounding-board, those of harps are strung in a plane perpendicular to the sounding-board. The longer strings of lower pitch are set at a greater distance from the sounding-board than the shorter ones. Unlike lyres, harps have no bridge over which the strings are strung; rather, their string-ends are fixed directly into the sounding-board. The strings of the harp were made to speak by the plucking of the finger without the aid of a plectrum, an execution termed *psallein*, from which word is derived our psalterion or psaltery. Other harps or psalteries were, in addition to the triangular harp, also called "Phoenician" harp: pektis, magadis, klepsiamb, skindapse, and henneachord, or nine-stringed harp.

Lute-type instruments, such as the pandoura, monochord, and canon, are distinguished from lyres and harps in virtue of their having a long neck, or fingerboard, surmounting a resonating chest.[15] The strings are stretched vertically over the finger-board from a stationary bridge at one extremity to tuning-pegs at the other, these serving to alter the tension of the strings. Each string is capable of emitting more than one pitch by being pressed against the finger-board, or "stopped" by the fingers. In this way, each string can be shortened and its pitch raised accordingly.

Finally, among the wind instruments are those whose distinctive attributes prompted Nicomachus to set them aside as intermediate. These are the transverse, or plagiauloi, and the photinxes. Both were held in the same manner as the modern flute, but unlike the flute, they were reed-blown instruments, the reeds contained in a mouth-piece set in the side of the air column. The sweetness of their timbre was apparently proverbial,[16] but strangely enough, if one were to judge by the rarity of their appearance in artistic representations, they seem to have been little cultivated in classical times.

Notes to Chapter 4

1. Jan, 241.7.

2. *Vors.* 47B1; DK, 432.10–433.1.

3. *Apud* Theon (Hiller, 50.5–9).

4. *Apud* Theon (Hiller, 50.9–12).

5. *De anima* 420a4–9. Thus, Burkert, p. 382, n. 55: "What is worked out in detail in Aristotle becomes a pithy definition for the 'Pythagoreans.'"

6. *De anima* 419b19–20.

7. *Timaeus* 67B2–5.

8. Jan, 149.6–7.

9. Jan, 149.6–11.

10. Mersenne, a Minorite friar, was the first to express mathematically the laws of the transverse vibration of strings. In so doing, he proved that the frequency of a stretched string is inversely proportional to its length; directly proportional to the square root of the tension; inversely proportional to the diameter of the string; and inversely proportional to the mass (and weight) of unit length of the string. The discovery of these relations was made independently by Mersenne's contemporary, Galileo. See Levin (1980), 206, n. 2.

11. The literature on ancient instruments is vast and comprehensive. Most useful in connection with those mentioned by Nicomachus is C. Sachs, *The History of Musical Instruments* (New York, 1940). The most important work written thus far on the aulos in all its permutations and manifestations is by K. Schlesinger, *The Greek Aulos* (London, 1939). On strings, we are now fortunate to have the critical study by W. Maas and J. M. Snyder, *Stringed Instruments of Ancient Greece* (New Haven and London, 1989).

12. Jan, 266.2–17.

13. Curiously enough, Maas and Snyder, in the work cited in note 11, make no mention of the spadix. That the spadix was a post-classical foreign import is to be inferred from its inclusion among a list of exotic instruments by the scholar and rhetorician of the second century C.E., Pollux, in his *Onomasticon* 4.59. Its earliest mention is by Quintilian (first century C.E.) as cited in the commentary to this chapter. An inscriptional notice (*SEG* 4. 61), perhaps from the first

century C.E., refers to a spadix made of silver, hence suggestive of a richly-wrought and intricately designed instrument. Otherwise, nothing at all is known of this censured stringed instrument.

14. *Institutio Oratoria* 1.10.31. Quintilian is, of course, adhering in this case to the strictures laid down by Plato in *Rep.* 399C10ff. There, Plato explains that instruments possessing more than seven or eight strings are capable of modulating into all the modes (*panarmonia*) and this, he maintains, leads to a corruption of music and the souls of those exposed to it. Instruments should therefore be constructed so as to produce only the two modes: Dorian and Phrygian.

15. Because the monochord and canon were, like modern guitars, provided with a finger-board upon which marks (like frets) could be placed, indicating the measurements of string length required for the production of desired pitches, they were ideally suited for acoustic experimentation. In fact, Aristides Quintilianus, a theorist of late antiquity, says in his *De Musica* 3.2 (Winnington-Ingram 97.3–4) that Pythagoras' very last words, just before he died, were to exhort his disciples to use the monochord in their researches. Of the lute-type instruments mentioned by Nicomachus, the pandoura was the most ancient, having been used by the Egyptians as early as the New Kingdom (c. 1570 B.C.E.). See H. G. Farmer, "The Music of Ancient Egypt," in *NOH*, pp. 273–74.

16. Thus, Theocritus *Id.* 20.28–29 associated it with other bucolic instruments of gentle timbre:

My song is sweet whether I sing to the syrinx,
or croon to the aulos or to the donax,
or to the plagiaulos.

Chapter 5

Pythagoras, by adding the eighth string to the seven-stringed lyre, instituted the attunement of the octave

PYTHAGORAS is the first one who—in order that the middle note, when combined itself with both extremes through conjunction, might not produce the consonance of a fourth only, a fourth with hypate at one extreme, and with nete at the other; and in order that we might be able to envisage a more varied scheme, the extremes themselves producing with one another the most satisfying consonance, that is, the octave in a double ratio, which could not result from the two tetrachords—intercalated an eighth note, which he fitted between mese and paramese and separated it from mese by a whole-tone and from paramese by a semi-tone. The result was that the string which was formerly paramese in the heptachord, still being the third string calculating from nete, is called trite and is situated in just this position; the intercalated string, on the other hand, is the fourth string calculating from nete and forms with it the consonance of a fourth, which is the consonance mese formed originally with hypate. The whole-tone between both these two strings, mese and the intercalated string which is named after the former paramese, to whichever tetrachord it is added, whether to the one that is contingent on hypate, in which case it is relatively high in pitch, or to the one contingent on nete, in which case it is relatively deep in pitch, will produce the consonance of a fifth, which is a system of both the tetrachord itself and the added whole tone. Thus the hemiolic ratio [3:2] of the fifth is found to be a system composed of the epitritic ratio [4:3] and of the sesquioctave ratio [9:8]. The whole-tone then is in a sesquioctave ratio.

Commentary 5

BY THE time of Pythagoras (sixth century B.C.E.), tradition had so hallowed the seven-stringed lyre, or heptachord, that any attempt to tamper with the number of its strings was looked upon as a sacrilege. The number seven in itself was considered sacred, as being manifested in all those objects which the ancients venerated: the seven planets, the seven sages, the seventh day of the month Bysios (Apollo's birthday), the seven gates of Thebes, and even the seven vowels of the Greek language, "which are not to be spoken aloud by wise men."[1]

To be sure, the lyre did not always have seven strings; there is a much earlier stage of the lyre, associated with Linos, a son of Apollo. According to legend, Linos had learned from his father the art of the trichord—the three stringed lyre. Sometime thereafter he added a fourth string—the lichanos or "fore-finger" string—and thus invented the four-stringed lyre, the earliest tetrachord. It was from the limits between the highest- and the lowest-pitched strings of this tetrachord—the fourth or "the first and most elementary consonance," as Nicomachus calls it in Chapter 12, p. 173—that all the musical scales of ancient Greek music eventually developed.[2]

The first great stage in the subsequent development of music—the first *katastasis*, as it came to be called—is assigned by the unanimous consent of our sources to the musician, Terpander of Antissa on Lesbos. Born about 710 B.C.E., and living well into the seventh century, Terpander's contributions to the formation of Greek music were so significant and lasting that by Nicomachus' time his name had assumed a mythological status. Terpander was all things to music: a singer, a composer, and an instrumentalist; he was also a poet, an instrument builder, an inventor of the barbitos, a musical theorist of great insight, a compositional innovator, and a winner at the Pythian competition four times in succession.[3] Perhaps his most lasting contribution was the transformation of the four-stringed lyre to the instrument which became institutionalized by tradition, i.e. the heptachord.[4] In two lines of his hexameter verse that have come down to us, he presents his reasons for creating that instrument:

74

We love no more our four-toned song,
And will sing new hymns to our seven-toned phorminx.

As described by Nicomachus in Chapter 3, this seven-toned heptachord comprised two tetrachords of identical form, each one spanning the most elementary concord, the fourth, and both joined together on the note mese.[5] In the present chapter Nicomachus relates how and why Pythagoras succeeded in doing what had to that time been forbidden all musicians to do, namely, extend the reach of the heptachord from its minor seventh limits to a full octave, in this way transforming the heptachord into an octachord. Although it remained for Pythagoras to succeed in this endeavor, it is not as though others had not earlier attempted what he in fact accomplished. Indeed, Terpander himself is reported to have devised a way of playing an octave on his instrument without having to add the forbidden eighth string:

> Why is the octave called *diapason* [lit.: extending through all the notes] instead of *diocto* [lit.: extending through eight notes] in answer to its number of notes, in the same way we call the fourth *diatettaron* [lit.: extending through four notes] and the fifth *diapente* [lit.: extending through five notes]? Is it because there were anciently seven strings and then Terpander removed trite and added nete? For this reason the octave was called *diapason* and not *diocto*, for it was comprised of seven notes.[6]

According to this description, Terpander's solution to the problem of the forbidden eighth string was to remove his B♮ string—the trite of the conjunct tetrachord—and add the octave string, E[l], yielding a scale of E F G A C D E[l]. While this arrangement left a gap of a minor third between A and C in the scale, it seems to have enhanced, rather than diminished, the Dorian character of Terpander's compositions. For Terpander's new octave note came to be called the "Dorian nete."[7] In striving for an octave note, other musicians were apparently much less observant of the ancient tradition: simply adding an eighth string to the existing seven and producing thereby what was considered a hybrid kind of Mixolydian music. To the conservatively trained ears of the Argives, alterations like these were so offensive that they assessed with fines those musicians who presumed to tamper with the heptachord's proper nature:[8]

> In ancient times, then, since their prime concern was with character, people valued above all the dignity and simplicity which was a feature of ancient music. Thus the Argives are said to have once laid down a penalty for breaches in the rules of music, and to have imposed a fine on the first man who tried to use more than the seven strings normally current among them and who attempted to modulate into Mixolydian.[9]

Guilty of similar infractions against the canons of music were Simonides of Cos who, as Pliny the Elder reported,[10] blatantly broke the rule: *octavam Simonides addidit*, and the otherwise unknown countryman of Pythagoras, Lycaon of Samos, who did no less according to Boethius:[11] *His octavam Samius Lycaon adiunxit*. In addition, Nicomachus in Chapter 11, p. 154 assigns the introduction of an eighth note to certain unnamed musicians who, he says, were seeking ways to "vary the attunement" of the ancient heptachord.[12]

Only Pythagoras escaped censure for adding an eighth string to the ancient and venerated lyre. To a great extent this was because, as the revered master and religious prophet, every act of his was felt by the ancients to have a special affinity with divine revelation or universal truth. But in addition, as Nicomachus in this chapter attempts to show, Pythagoras had a scientific and well-motivated reason for extending the heptachord. Whereas the purpose of practicing musicians who attempted such extension was to achieve greater gratification of the senses, Pythagoras' purpose was to teach man the unifying principle and the immutable laws of *harmonia*. In pursuing this goal, therefore, Pythagoras was appealing not to man's untrustworthy and corruptible senses but, instead, to his highest powers—those of the rational intellect. Thus, as the ancients saw it, Pythagoras altered the heptachord solely to engage man's intellect in the proper "fitting together" (*harmonia*) of the mathematical proportions:[13]

But the noble Pythagoras did not wish music to be judged according to the senses, for he said that its virtue could be apprehended only by the intellect; for that reason, he did not judge it on the basis of his ear, but on that of the *harmonia* of proportion. He thought it sufficient therefore to limit the study of music to the octave.[14]

Pythagoras' alteration of the heptachord produced results that have reverberated through the centuries: not only did it lay the groundwork for the subsequent development of the Greek musical scale systems, but it also established the basis for all future harmonic and acoustical theory. As a musical act, it was sublimely simple; as a mathematical production, however, it was incalculably profound. Its simplicity consists in this: Pythagoras took the two tetrachords of the heptachord and separated them by a whole-tone. The Argives, it will be remembered, had been deeply offended by those musicians who, in adding an octave note to the scale, violated the norms of tetrachordal usage and produced something that sounded to them like a Mixolydian type of music:

E   F   G   A   B♭   C   D   E^|

To the ears of the Argives, the interval between B♭ and the upper E^| was anomalous; it was not the true fourth that they expected to hear. Pythagoras solved the problem by maintaining the basic form or *schema* of each tetrachord, while at the same time separating the one from the other by a whole-tone. The established tetrachordal *schema* is then: semi-tone, whole-tone, whole-tone. To maintain this *schema*, Pythagoras had only to raise B♭ to B natural and add the octave-note E^|. This set for all time the fundamental form of the Dorian scale from which all the Greek musical systems eventually developed:[15]

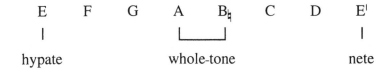

E   F   G   A   B♮   C   D   E^|
| |___| |
hypate   whole-tone   nete

In his description of the steps that Pythagoras took to achieve this scale, Nicomachus created enough confusion to found and foster all the scholarly debate and commentary that have accumulated ever after. For Nicomachus does not make clear what Pythagoras' reform essentially consisted in, namely, the insertion of a whole-tone between tetrachords. On the contrary, if we take him literally, we are led to believe that what Pythagoras in fact effected was the insertion of an eighth string between mese (A) and what Nicomachus called paramese of the ancient heptachord (B♭), clearly an impossibility.[16] For to accomplish this result, Pythagoras would first have had to force the tetrachords apart. Thus, as Nicomachus has it, the string which was third from the top in the heptachord, i.e. B♭, or paramese, was now shifted upward to C (trite), and the new string, B♮, came to be called paramese. The critical note E', however, seems to have materialized by itself, for Nicomachus makes no mention of it. Yet it is this note, namely E', which Pythagoras had most likely added to the heptachord, rather than the note which, according to Nicomachus, was inserted between mese (A) and paramese (B♭). Nicomachus' entire analysis of the new scale, however, depends on the presence of the upper octave note E'. For, as he has it, the entire scale incorporates a fifth, a fourth, and a whole-tone. And this can only be possible with hypate as E, mese as A, paramese as B♮, and nete as E':

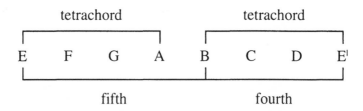

In this kind of musical system then, it follows that the whole-tone which functions as a disjunction (*diazeuxis*) between the tetrachords is, as Nicomachus says, high in pitch relative to the lower tetrachord, and low in pitch relative to the upper tetrachord. Moreover, adding a whole-tone to either tetrachord produces a

fifth. As a consequence, the fifth in the ratio of 3:2 is mathematically equivalent to a fourth plus a whole-tone; or, to put it another
way, a fourth subtracted from a fifth leaves a whole-tone:

$$3 : 2 \div 4 : 3 = 9 : 8$$

Notes to Chapter 5

1. Nicomachus, *Excerpt 6*, p. 194.

2. In Chapter 11 Nicomachus explains how the scale systems developed from the combination of tetrachords by conjunction (as in the ancient heptachord) and by disjunction (as in the octachord). In all such sequences the original form of the diatonic tetrachord was maintained: semi-tone, whole-tone, whole-tone.

3. Pindar *apud* Athenaeus 635D.

4. Seven-stringed lyres were used as far back as 1400–1100 B.C.E. in the period known as Late Minoan III. This is evident from various archeological specimens. Most celebrated among these is the stone sarcophagus from Hagia Triada now in the Heraklion museum on Crete. Appearing on this sarcophagus in its most complete form, the lyre most certainly has seven strings (see Maas and Snyder, pp. 2–3). On Terpander's introduction of the heptachord, see Comotti, pp. 16–17. On the implications of Terpander's innovations, see Winnington-Ingram (1958), pp. 14–16.

5. See above, Chapter 3, p. 47. The middle note, mese, was assigned by Nicomachus to the Sun and formed the point of conjunction, or *synaphe*, between two tetrachords of the same *schema*, or form, namely, that described in note 2 above. A fourteenth century C.E. Byzantine theorist, Manuel Bryennius, who made much use of Nicomachus in his *Harmonica*, says in this connection that this heptachordal scale was actually devised by Hermes himself in imitation of the tones produced by the seven planets (*Harm.* 1.362; Jonker, 56.12–21).

6. Ps.-Aristotle, *Problem* 19.32.

7. Ps.-Plutarch, *De mus.* ch. 28; 1140F.

8. Ps.-Plutarch, *De mus.* ch. 37; 1144E–F.

9. Translation by Barker, I (1984), p. 244. As Barker explains in note 238, if to the two conjunct tetrachords of the heptachord a whole-tone is added at the treble, a Mixolydian octave structure is formed. In other words, the structure of the Mixolydian mode as regularized by Aristoxenus is in all essentials "a conjunct scale of Dorian form, completing the octave with an additional tone at the top." Cf. Barker, I (1984), pp. 221–22, n. 113.

10. *Nat. Hist.* 7.204.

11. *De inst. mus.* 1.20 (Friedlein, 207.8): *His octavam Samius Lycaon adiunxit.* In his translation of Boethius' *De institutione musica*, Bower, p. 32, n. 107, presents an interesting theory regarding this Lycaon from Samos. He suggests that Lycaon is a cult name for Pythagoras, that it is related to the Etruscan *lucomo*, "a word associated with both insanity and divine powers." Hence, Boethius' words, Samius Lycaon, may be a veiled reference to Pythagoras himself.

12. Jan, 257.18–22.

13. Ps.-Plutarch, *De mus.* ch. 37; 1145A.

14. For Pythagoras and his disciples, the word *harmonia* meant "octave" in the sense of an "attunement" which manifests within its limits both the proper "fitting together" of the concordant intervals, fourth and fifth, and the difference between them, the whole-tone. Moreover, as Pythagoras proved, whatever can be said of any one octave holds true for all octaves. For every octave, no matter what pitch range it encompasses, repeats itself without variation throughout the entire pitch range of music. It is thus with reason that Pythagoras thought it sufficient to limit the study of music to the octave.

15. See Mountford (1920), 28–29, who observes that within a hundred years of the time when Pythagoras effected this first break with the old order, stringed instruments had increased to at least eleven strings.

16. No one before Nicomachus ever applied the name "paramese" to the note B♭ in the heptachord. On the contrary, they called this note "trite", the third note from the treble in the conjunct (*synemmenon*) tetrachord. As if to justify his own application of "paramese" to B♭, Nicomachus alleges that Pythagoras' alteration of the heptachord to an octachord occasioned a change in terminology. While Boethius accepted Nicomachus' use of "paramese" as historically factual, he nonetheless added: *quae etiam trite dicitur*, "the note which we now call trite" (*De inst. mus.* 1.20; Friedlein 206.27–29). As for himself, Boethius thought it best in this connection to use both names interchangeably for B♭: *paramese vel trite*. In all then, the only theorists who called B♭ "paramese" are those who copied Nicomachus, namely, the Byzantines Manuel Bryennius and Georges Pachymeres.

In attempting to make sense of this passage, Jacques Chailley (1956), pp. 76ff., suggested that Nicomachus' paramese should be construed as the note C in a gapped scale like that of Terpander, and that Pythagoras inserted the note B♮ between mese (A) and Terpander's paramese (C). And that this occasioned a change in terminology of paramese for B♮ and trite for C.

Chapter 6

How the numerical proportions
of the notes were discovered

THE INTERVAL of strings comprising a fourth, that of a fifth, and that formed by the union of both, which is called an octave, as well as that of the whole-tone lying between the two tetrachords, was confirmed by Pythagoras to have this numerical quantity by means of a certain method which he discovered. One day he was deep in thought and seriously considering whether it could be possible to devise some kind of instrumental aid for the ears which would be firm and unerring, such as vision obtains through the compass and the ruler or the *dioptra*; or touch obtains with the balance-beam or the system of measures. While thus engaged, he walked by a smithy and, by divine chance, heard the hammers beating out iron on the anvil and giving off in combination sounds which were most harmonious with one another, except for one combination. He recognized in these sounds the consonance of the octave, the fifth and the fourth. But he perceived that the interval between the fourth and the fifth was dissonant in itself but was otherwise complementary to the greater of these two consonances. Elated, therefore, since it was as if his purpose was being divinely accomplished, he ran into the smithy and found by various experiments that the difference of sound arose from the weight of the hammers, but not from the force of the blows, nor from the shapes of the hammers, nor from the alteration of the iron being forged. After carefully examining the weights of the hammers and their impacts, which were identical, he went home.

He planted a single stake diagonally in the walls in order that no difference might arise from this procedure or, in short, that no variation might be detected from the use of several stakes, each with its own peculiar properties. From this stake he suspended four strings of the same material and made of an equal number of strands, equal in thickness and of equal torsion. He then attached a weight to the bottom of each string, having suspended each by each in succession. When he arranged that the lengths of the strings should be exactly equal, he alternately struck two strings simultaneously and found the aforementioned consonances, a different consonance being produced by a different pair of strings.

He found that the string stretched by the greatest weight produced, when compared with that stretched by the smallest, an octave. The weight on one string was twelve pounds, while that on the other was six pounds. Being therefore in a double ratio [2:1], it produced the octave, the ratio being evidenced by the weights themselves. Again, he found that the string under the greatest tension compared with that next to the string under the least tension (the string stretched by a weight of eight pounds), produced a fifth. Hence he discovered that this string was in a hemiolic ratio [3:2] with the string under the greatest tension, the ratio in which the weights also stood to one another. Then he found that the string stretched by the greatest weight, when compared with that which was next to it in weight, being under a tension of nine pounds, produced a fourth, analogous to the weights. He concluded, therefore, that this string was undoubtedly in an epitritic ratio [4:3] with the string under the greatest tension and that this same string was by nature in a hemiolic ratio with the string under the least tension (for this is the case with the ratio of 9 to 6). In a similar way, the string neighboring on that under the least tension, that is, the string stretched by a weight of eight pounds, compared with that stretched by a weight of six pounds, was in an epitritic ratio, but it was in a hemiolic ratio with the string stretched by a weight of twelve pounds.

Then that interval which is between the fifth and the fourth, that is, the interval by which the fifth is greater than the fourth, was confirmed to be in a sesquioctave ratio [9:8], which is as 9 is to 8. And either way it was proved that the octave is a system consisting of the fifth and the fourth in conjunction, just as the double ratio consists of the hemiolic ratio and the epitritic, as for example, 12, 8, and 6; or conversely, it consists of the fourth and the fifth, just as the double ratio consists of the epitritic ratio and the hemiolic, as for example, 12, 9, and 6, in such order.

And having inured his hand and his hearing to the suspended

weights and having established on their basis that ratio of their relations, he ingeniously transferred the bond, which fastened all the strings, from the diagonal stake to the bridge of the instrument, which he called *chordotonon* or string-stretcher, and he transferred the amount of tension on the strings analogous to the weights, to the commensurate turning of the tuning pegs set in the upper part of the instrument. Using this as a standard and as it were an infallible pointer, he extended the test henceforward to various instruments, namely, to the percussion on plates, to auloi and panpipes, to monochords and triangular harps, and the like. And in all of these he found consistent and unchanging, the determination by number.

He called the note partaking of the number 6, hypate, that of the number 8, mese, this number being in an epitritic proportion with the number 6; that of the number 9, he called paramese, which is higher than mese by a whole tone and what is more, stands in a sesquioctave proportion with it; that of 12, he called nete. Filling out the intervening intervals in the diatonic genus with analogous notes, he thus subordinated the octachord to the consonant numbers, the double ratio [2:1], the hemiolic [3:2], the epitritic [4:3], and the difference between them, the sesquioctave [9:8].

Commentary 6

AFTER threading her way through Chapter 5 with its self-consciously long opening sentence and its almost intentionally obscure account of Pythagoras' alteration of the heptachord, Nicomachus' learned reader must have been pleasantly surprised to come upon the complete change of style that informs Chapter 6. Indeed, as if to make up for the theoretical obfuscations of Chapter 5 (brought about, perhaps, by the distractions of travel), Nicomachus offers his reader in Chapter 6 a story about Pythagoras that is nothing if not clear and easy to follow. Whatever his reader may have felt about it, one thing is certain: she had to have been the very first person in recorded history to read this story in complete form. For as far as we can ascertain, no Greek-speaking person had ever committed the story to writing before Nicomachus.[1] Once recorded, it was passed along from Nicomachus to Adrastus, Gaudentius, and Censorinus, to Iamblichus, Macrobius, and Fulgentius, to Chalcidius, Boethius, and Isidore of Seville—gathering celebrity in transit and charming its hearers wherever it was told.[2] It exists today as a musical artifact in the *Air con Variazioni* of Handel's *Harpsichord Suite No. V*, a movement commonly known as "The Harmonious Blacksmith." Hearing that *Air* today, one cannot but think of Pythagoras walking by the smithy, his ears filled with the anvil's ringing tones and his mind transfixed by their unfolding implications. For like Pythagoras' musical discovery, Handel's *Air* begins simply, but as it proceeds through the *Variazioni* it not only illuminates itself, but also yields in the end an infinite series of ideas.

Nicomachus seems to have brought the story of Pythagoras and "the harmonious blacksmith" to his reader in much the same form as that in which he originally heard it. For in retelling it he made no attempt to address its many improbabilities. On the contrary, he seems to have preserved it exactly as it must have reached him, with all its marvels intact. This has earned him the censure of modern scholars and mathematicians but, interestingly enough, those ancient savants who handed down his version of the tale (sometimes verbatim) obviously accepted it from him without demur.[3] Yet they too must have noticed certain of its incongruities. Indeed, one has only to try duplicating the experiment detailed by Nicomachus in this chapter to discover that it does not work, that the results adduced by Nicomachus simply cannot be obtained. This is primarily because attaching weights to equal strings, as Nicomachus represents Pythagoras doing, will not produce the musical notes that he alleges Pythagoras to have produced. Assuming then that Iamblichus or Gaudentius or Boethius, or anyone else for that matter, had tried to duplicate the experiment with weighted strings, each one of them would sooner or later have come upon its flaws.[4] If they have registered no complaint or criticism of the experiment in their retelling of it, it is therefore because they probably took Nicomachus' story for what it is: a folk-tale, and thus not to be analyzed but to be countenanced for bearing witness to an actual and momentous event: the discovery by Pythagoras of the mathematical bases of music.[5]

As it stands, Nicomachus' tale has antecedents that are very ancient and which, at the same time, are decidedly Near Eastern in tone. Porphyry suggests as much when he connects Pythagoras with the "Idaean Daktyls" of Crete. These *daktyloi*, the dwarfish smiths and masters of all arts and crafts, were said by ancient Phrygian chroniclers to have worked originally for the great Asian goddess Rhea Kybele, or Magna Mater as she came to be known by the Romans. Moreover, it was reported of these Nibelungen-like *daktyloi* that they discovered in the different notes of their anvils the mathematical bases of music. As Porphyry has it, Pythagoras not only visited the Cretan cave of these *daktyloi*, but he stayed long enough with them (twenty days, to be exact) to have learned all their secrets, musical and otherwise.[6]

Legends aside, Pythagoras, in addition to all else that has been said of him, was an imposing musician. He was also the first musician to recognize the therapeutic value of music and the ethical effects it produced on the soul. Such being the case, he did not hesitate to prescribe music instead of drugs for specific illnesses; he even enlisted music's aid against the soul's aberrations.[7] It was said that he preferred the lyre to the aulos because the quality of the latter was in his estimation *hybristikos* (insolent) and *panegyrikos* (ostentatious). The lyre, on the other hand, he regarded as an instrument especially suited for accompanying hymns to the gods.[8] Not surprisingly then, Pythagoras focused his attention on the lyre and the various tunings of which it was capable. He must have spent many an hour experimenting with one tuning or another before he came up with that described by Nicomachus in Chapter 5: the Dorian octachord. Having achieved this innovative scale, Pythagoras, being the intense musician we know him to have been, would have concerned himself to certify that his two new fifths were absolutely identical and that his two absolutely identical fourths were separated from one another by a true whole-tone between mese (A) and paramese (B). In making this effort, however, he had only his ear as a guide, scarcely the most trustworthy instrument, even for a being as superior as Pythagoras. What he trusted in these endeavors far more than his ear, however, was his mind. And in this regard he taught his disciples to do likewise:

> For the mind is what sees all things
> and hears all things; everything else
> is deaf and blind.[9]

In order to provide the mind with accurate information, however, the contribution of the senses had to be implemented by instruments or tools of some sort. When provided with information buttressed in this way, the mind would then be in a position to exercise its own function, i.e. to "see all things and hear all things." It was in this way that one arrived at the truth, namely, those universal laws that govern all reality, whether seen or heard. On Pythagoras' approach, such laws were discoverable not by the unaided senses, but through the mind's instrumentality.

As matters stood in what concerned the eye, the mind drew support from the fact that there was available sufficient assistance from instruments to provide it with accurate and trustworthy information. In particular, as Nicomachus explains, the eye could rely on the compass or *diabetes* which, as the term literally denotes, is "the straddler" that stands with its legs apart and assists the eye to calibrate things. The eye could consult also the *kanon* or straight-edge ruler that measures distances, as well as the *dioptra*, literally, the "see-through" instrument that measures the size of horizontal or vertical angles. And the simple scale or balance-beam (*zugon*), the last instrument mentioned by Nicomachus, offered to the sense of touch the assistance it needed for assessing the accurate weight of things.[10]

Unlike the eye (and the hand), however, the ear could rely on no instrument at all when it came to determining the difference between musical pitches. In other words, without the assistance of a tool of some sort, the ear could make only rough estimates of the size of one interval or another.[11] That being the case, the ear—even the ear of Pythagoras—could not provide accurate data of the kind that Pythagoras would need to arrive at the truth—the truth in this particular case being the principle according to which the Dorian *harmonia* was constructed. Unaided by any acoustical tool, Pythagoras' ear could not provide scientifically reliable evidence. Accordingly, his mind was defeated in its effort to discover the truth of what he was hearing in his lyre strings. In the final analysis, this meant that where music was concerned there could be no truth—no truth, that is, in the Pythagorean sense of an eternal and exact ideal against which all the audible phenomena could be measured.

Whether Pythagoras discovered the truth he was seeking when, in one of his earlier incarnations he visited the Idaean Daktyls,[12] or whether he came upon it on his own, as Nicomachus reports, there can be no doubt that Pythagoras did in fact discover something monumental, something so important that it altered the course of mathematical science and laid the groundwork for a whole new science, that of acoustical physics. Though it was inspired by an ecstatic kind of revelation in the smithy, Pythagoras' vision of acoustical truth was essentially mind-driven, and it issued in the ordered beauty of mathematical knowledge. It was a knowledge obtained by thought and, as such, it gave proof that thought is superior to the senses. But, as Nicomachus testifies, the eternal acoustic truth obtained by thought, from which all sense-driven knowledge was believed by Pythagoras to fall short, had to have been preceded by tests of a decidedly empirical sort.[13]

With that consideration clearly in mind, Nicomachus presents Pythagoras on the threshold of his dazzling discovery, his mind troubled, his thinking intense, as he searches for a yardstick, as it were, to make known the unknowns of acoustical nature. As the story goes—beginning with Nicomachus and proceeding down through the centuries—it was Pythagoras' good fortune which, in directing him to walk by the harmonious smithy, brought to him what all his profound cogitations could not succeed in achieving. For there, issuing from the smith's anvil were the ringing sounds of pitches in relations that were identical to those which he produced on the strings of the lyre: the octave, the fifth, and the fourth, all intervals which were harmonious to his ear. The one combination that sounded discordant matched the sound of the whole-tone that he had inserted between the two tetrachords of his original seven-stringed lyre, the heptachord. The pitches that Pythagoras heard in the smithy were therefore:

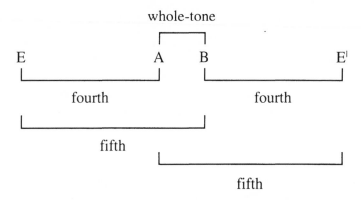

Once in the smithy, Pythagoras found that four hammers of different weights were responsible for producing the four different pitches that he heard. Thus he determined that the weight of the hammers and nothing else—not the force or impact of the hammers, not the iron being forged, not the anvil itself, not the shape of the hammers—was the factor accountable for the differences in pitch. And Nicomachus, as if to emphasize this remarkable fact, uses almost every word in his lexicon to denote weight and nothing but weight: *ongkos* (ὄγκος), *sekoma* (σήκωμα), *exartema* (ἐξάρτημα), *holke* (ὁλκή), *bare* (βάρη), *stathmon* (σταθμόν), *brithos* (βρῖθος). From this point on in Nicomachus' account, the emphasis is largely on the factor of weight. Thus we read that Pythagoras' first step in setting up his experiment was to fashion four weights corresponding to those of the smith's hammers. His next step was to position a stake across the angle formed by two walls and secure it firmly in the walls. From this stake he suspended four strings that were equal to one another in all respects except as to their length. After suspending a weight to the end of each string, Pythagoras then made sure to adjust the strings so that they would be equal in length. He then plucked two strings at the same time and found that they sounded pitches in the same relations as those he heard coming from the smithy. Pythagoras concluded from this that it was the different weights—these being of the values 12, 9, 8, and 6—that determined the variations in the pitches he heard.

In an important shift of focus, Nicomachus then goes on to correlate the tension (ἐπίτασις) on the strings with the value of each of the weights. And the results, he claims, are that an octave is produced by two strings weighted with 12 and 6 units, the ratio of their relations being 2:1; a fifth by weights of 12 and 8 units, the ratio of their relations being 3:2; and a fourth by weights of 12 and 9 units, the ratio of their relations being 4:3. And the discordant whole-tone was found by Pythagoras to be produced by the two strings weighted with units of 9 and 8, the ratio of their relations being that of the sesquioctave. All these things being so, it could now be demonstrated that an octave, being of the proportion 2:1, is compounded of the fifth (3:2) and the fourth (4:3), as in 12:8:6; or conversely, it is a compound of the fourth (4:3) and the fifth (3:2), as in 12:9:6.

After testing his four-string contraption over and over, Pythagoras presumably refined it sufficiently to produce what eventually became an important acoustical tool, i.e. the monochord.[14] With this implement Pythagoras could duplicate everything he had learned to that point. If we take Nicomachus literally, the contraption from which the monochord evolved was a four-stringed lute-like arrangement consisting of a bridge or *chordotone*, literally "string-stretcher," over which the strings were extended, each wrapped around its own tuning-peg. All that remained was for Pythagoras to turn each peg so as to produce on each string an amount of tension that was equivalent to the weights on the suspended strings. Accordingly, with tension as his standard of measure, Pythagoras demonstrated that the strings under the least tension produced the lower pitches, while those under the greatest tension produced the higher pitches. This is reflected in Nicomachus' assignment of the numbers to the pitches:[15]

hypate (lowest pitch or E)	6 (smallest number)
mese (middle pitch or A)	8
paramese (next to the middle pitch or B)	9
nete (highest pitch or E')	12 (largest number)

Within these notes are comprised the structural components (octave, fifth, and fourth) of the Dorian octachord, Pythagoras' own musical innovation. It remained only for Pythagoras to fill in the intervening notes of the scale to produce the complete diatonic octave. With this Nicomachus ends the chapter.

There are in Nicomachus' account two fundamental flaws; the first concerns percussion, the second, tension. To begin with, a single anvil struck by four different hammers would not behave as Nicomachus has it—that is, it would not sound four different pitches. On the contrary, it would give off one and the same pitch. This is because pitch variation produced by percussion depends on the object struck, in this case, the anvil, and not on the objects doing the striking, here, the hammers. For an anvil, if set into vibration by a hammer blow, functions exactly like a bell, a cymbal, or a metal plate, the pitch of each object depending on its size, composition, and shape.[16] Thus if, as Nicomachus has it, Pythagoras extended his tests to metal plates, he would have discovered this most basic fact about the role of percussion in the production of sound. Interestingly enough, there are reports of similar experiments conducted by a follower of Pythagoras, namely, Hippasus of Metapontum. Using four bronze discs of identical diameter, their thicknesses being of the proportions 4:3, 3:2, and 2:1, Hippasus is said to have produced the consonances fourth, fifth, and octave, respectively. What is more, when Hippasus presented his four well-tuned discs to Glaukos of Rhegium, a musician of great repute, Glaukos could actually play a tune on them.[17] The second flaw—that concerning tension—is said to have been discovered in the nineteenth century by a French scholar, Théodore H. Martin, who pointed out that the ratios detailed by Nicomachus do not accurately express the relation between a string's pitch and the amount of tension required to produce the pitch variations assumed by him.[18] For the peculiar relation that obtains between tension and frequency of vibration requires that the latter, the frequency, be the square root of the former, tension. This means that in order to raise the pitch of a string to an octave, the tension exerted on it must be four times greater than that producing the lower note. To produce a fifth, the tension must be two and a quarter times greater, and to produce a fourth, it must be one and seven-ninths greater. To put it another way, the relation of tension to frequency of vibration is expressed by 4:1 (octave), 9:4 (fifth), and 16:9 (fourth).Thus, anyone attempting to duplicate Pythagoras' experiment with weighted strings would have discovered that the intervals produced thereby fall considerably short of an octave, fifth, and fourth.

Although Marin Mersenne is credited with having first discovered the true relation between tension and frequency of vibration in the seventeenth century, there is evidence that Ptolemy, the great astronomer, mathematician, and harmonician, was in fact the first one who tried to duplicate the experiment detailed by Nicomachus. After using weights to stretch the strings, Ptolemy concluded that "there was indeed a rise in the pitch of the strings, but it was inconsistent with the ratios of the weights."[19]

In sum then, the smith's hammers, the weights attached to the strings, and their supposed equivalents—tensions on the strings—have no place in the world of acoustical fact. They are in every respect fabulous elements in a long-standing legend. Nonetheless, they point to something that lies at the very center of Pythagorean thought—the notion of the corporeality of number. When, therefore, the Pythagoreans, under the impulse of Pythagoras' discovery of the mathematical bases of musical pitch, proceeded to construct the whole world out of numbers, it was in the final analysis because they conceived of numbers as having material substance. This concept is importantly emphasized by Nicomachus in his numerous and varied references to weight in this chapter. Of all the terms he uses in this respect, the one most commonly adopted by the Pythagoreans to signify individual numerical units is *ongkos* (ὄγκος).

Removing the factors weight and tension from Nicomachus' story, however, and replacing them with the single factor of string length proportion reveals the ultimate truth of Pythagoras' discovery: the numerical ratios are absolutely correct and involve no acoustical error when taken in terms of string-length proportion—the very terms which Nicomachus consistently uses in the balance of his treatise.[20]

Notes to Chapter 6

1. Despite the weight of the tradition that assigns to Pythagoras the mathematical determination of the octave, fifth and fourth, the fact remains that before Nicomachus there is no definitive evidence to support the claim. On this problem, see Levin (1975), pp. 68–69.

2. Of all these writers, only Adrastus (second century C.E.) comes close to Nicomachus in date. The others named range from the third century C.E. (Censorinus and Gaudentius) to Boethius (sixth century C.E.) and Isidore (seventh century C.E.). Thus, one of the most surprising elements in the whole Pythagorean tradition is its inverse proportion between the amount of documentation and its date of origin. The fact is that the closer one approaches the era of Pythagoras himself, the sparser is the evidence concerning his activities. This condition derives quite possibly from the oath of secrecy that bound the earliest members of the Pythagorean school. Cf. Levin (1975), p. 74 for detailed references to the works of these authors in which Nicomachus' story reappears.

3. The account offered by Iamblichus in his *De vita Pyth.* 115–120 (Deubner, 66–69) is taken verbatim from that of Nicomachus.

4. As far as we can ascertain, Ptolemy is the only theorist who gives evidence of having tried the experiment outlined by Nicomachus. To be sure, he does not mention Nicomachus in this connection, but he shows himself to have been critical enough of the experiment to be familiar with its elaboration by Nicomachus. Cf. Levin (1980), 228–29.

5. Thus Burnet, p. 107: "They are not stories which any Greek mathematician could possibly have invented, but popular tales bearing witness to the existence of a real tradition that Pythagoras was the author of this momentous discovery."

6. This is reported by Porphyry, *Vita Pyth.* 17 (Nauck, 20.13–23).

7. See Iamblichus, *De vita Pyth.* 25.110 (Deubner, 63.14–65.15).

8. See Diogenes Laertius 8.24.

9. Iamblichus, *De vita Pyth.* 32.228 (Deubner, 122.15–16).

10. Plato, *Philebus* 56A3–C6, thus argues that music is of all the arts the least susceptible of accuracy and systematic study precisely because it lacks the proper tools of measurement such as those of

carpentry and shipbuilding. The tools mentioned by Plato in this connection are, interestingly, the same as those cited here by Nicomachus: the *kanon* and the *diabetes*. Not mentioned by Nicomachus are, in Plato's list, the *tornos*, a compass for drawing circles, and the *stathme*, the plumbline. If, therefore, as Nicomachus says, Pythagoras invented an instrument to assist the ear in the interests of accuracy, Plato, as is evident in this passage, knew nothing about it.

11. Thus Plato, *Rep.* 531A4–B4, has Glaukon deriding those musicians who had to tune their strings by sheer guesswork, using their ears instead of their minds and tormenting their strings by twisting the tuning pegs one way or another—all this to find the smallest of measurable intervals.

12. The doctrine of metempsychosis is very strong in the various accounts of Pythagoras' life. In Diogenes Laertius 8.4, for example, Pythagoras is reported to have once been the son of Hermes, then Euphorbus who was slain by Menelaus in the Trojan War. Before becoming Pythagoras, he was also Hermotimus and then Pyrrhus, a fisherman of Delos. Most important, when he finally became Pythagoras, he never forgot anything he ever learned in his previous incarnations.

13. Thus D. R. Fideler in Guthrie (1988), p. 47: "the harmonic proportion, according to legend discovered by Pythagoras, exists as a purely universal principle, but it would have never been discovered without empirical experimentation on the monochord."

14. On the monochord, see Fideler in Guthrie (1988), pp. 24–26. In addition to Nicomachus, other authorities ascribe the invention of the monochord to Pythagoras, as, for example, Diogenes Laertius 8.12 and Gaudentius, *Intro. Harm.* 11 (Jan, 341.12ff). According to Aristides Quintilianus, *De mus.* 3.2 (Winnington-Ingram, 97.3–7), Pythagoras' last words to his disciples before dying were to pursue their studies using the monochord since musical excellence could best be achieved through mental efforts instead of guesswork by ear. Interestingly enough, however, the monochord seems to have been unknown to both Plato and Aristotle. On the basis of historical evidence, its invention has been estimated as coming after 300 B.C.E. On this whole question, see Burkert, p. 375, n. 22.

15. The arrangement of the entire set of relations yields a kind of acoustical carpenter's square or *gnomon*, for which see D. R. Fideler in Guthrie (1988), pp. 22–24.

16. Thus Guthrie (1971), p. 223: "Beating a piece of iron on an anvil with hammers of different weights produces little or no difference in the pitch of the sounds." In order, therefore, for Pythagoras to have heard four different pitches issuing from the smithy, there would have had to be four different anvils involved in the production of the four different pitches.

17. This was reported by Aristoxenus (fr. 90 Wehrli). It is corroborated by Theon (Hiller, 59.4ff.), who also reports on an experiment conducted by Lasus of Hermione involving percussion on vases filled with varying amounts of water. See R. and D. Lawlor, p. 39. Glaukos of Rhegium should not be confused with Glaukon, Plato's brother, mentioned in note 11.

18. Th. H. Martin, *Études sur le Timée de Platon*, vol. I (Paris 1841), p. 391. Cf. Levin (1980), 220, n. 50. For Newton's explanation of the fallacy, see Godwin, *The Harmony of the Spheres*, pp. 305ff.

19. Ptolemy, *Harm.* 1.7 (Düring, 17.15–16).

20. Thus Burnet, p. 107: "On the other hand, the statement that he [Pythagoras] discovered the 'consonances' by measuring the lengths corresponding to them on the monochord is quite credible and involves no error in acoustics."

Chapter 7

On the division of the octave in the diatonic genus

THUS HE discovered, on the basis of a certain natural necessity, the progression in this diatonic genus from the lowest note to the highest. (For from this procedure he also revealed the structure of the chromatic and enharmonic genera, as it will be possible for me to show you some time later.) This diatonic genus appears, however, to comprehend by nature the degrees and progressions such as follow: semi-tone, a whole-tone, and then a whole-tone. And this is the system of a fourth, consisting of two whole-tones and the semi-tone, so-called. Then, by the addition of another whole-tone, namely, the intercalated whole-tone, the fifth results, being a system of three whole-tones and a semi-tone. Then next in order to this come a semi-tone, a whole-tone, and a whole-tone, being another system of a fourth, that is, another epitritic proportion. So that in the more ancient heptachord all the notes four removed from one another, starting from the lowest, were consonant throughout with each other by a fourth, the semi-tone occupying by transference the first, the middle, and the third place in the tetrachord.

In the Pythagorean octachord, however, whether it be composed of a tetrachord and a pentachord by conjunction, or of two tetrachords separated by a whole-tone from one another by disjunction, the progression by ascent will result in all the notes five removed from one another forming the consonance of a fifth with each other, the semitone as one advances, shifting into the four places, first, second, third, and fourth.

Commentary 7

ACCORDING to Nicomachus, it was Pythagoras' initial transformation of the heptachord into an octachord that led him to discover the mathematical laws determining the basic structure of the octave. With this transformation effected, Pythagoras, after experimentation on instruments of various sorts, could demonstrate that the octave is a *harmonia* or attunement of concordant intervals and that the mathematically fixed boundaries of these intervals add up to a ratio of 2:1, the ratio of an octave.[1] He proved that this was so by measuring the sounding-bodies of various instruments—of auloi, panpipes, discs and plates, and the string-lengths of harps, lyres, and lutes. Then, as he showed most clearly with the stringed instruments, when given any two stretched strings, if one be twice as long as the other, it will vibrate proportionally slower and produce a pitch an octave lower than the string half its length. Leaving then his experiments with musical instruments and turning to pure arithmetic, Pythagoras was able to prove that any two tetrachords whose extremes are in the proportion 4:3, and which are separated from one another by a whole-tone in the proportion 9:8, as in his newly-fashioned Dorian octachord, together add up to an octave: 4:3 x 4:3 x 9:8 = 144:72 or 2:1.

He could also prove in the same way—i.e. without consulting the dimensions of strings, air-columns, or plates, or listening to the results with his ear—that the fifth on his Dorian octachord, when added to a fourth, resulted in an octave: 3:2 x 4:3 = 12:6 or 2:1.

This meant that within the framework of any octave, no matter what its particular pitch range, there is a mathematically ordained place for the fourth, for the fifth, and for the whole-tone. That being the case, it was a simple mathematical matter to show that all of the ratios involved in the structure of the octave are comprehended by the single construct: 12:9::8:6.[2] For the Pythagoreans, this construct came to constitute the essential paradigm—of unity from multiplicity, of concinnity between opposites, in fact, of truth incarnate. Its peculiar power derived from the fact that it was the object not of the fallible senses but of pure thought. Reinforced as it was by mathematics, this abstract paradigm was for the Pythagoreans far more real than any sensible object could ever be since, as the very embodiment of truth, it existed not in time but in eternity.

Long before he discovered this truth, Pythagoras had practiced music, playing his lyre for the pleasure it gave, for the therapy it provided, and for the salutary influence it exerted on the soul. He knew music as Homer knew trees and birds.[3] Most of all, he knew those things in music which set the conditions for melody—conditions such that whatever happens melodically is musically natural—or, as Nicomachus has it, *physical*.[4] In other words, Pythagoras knew of music that beneath the endless diversity of melody, there are profound tonal similarities and radical musical certainties. Although his knowledge of these things was given sensorially, being derived exclusively from the testimony of his ear, there was, underlying this knowledge, the fundamental recognition that every tetrachord on which melody is based embodies the natural, i.e. *physical*, musical progression of semi-tone, whole-tone, whole-tone.[5]

When Pythagoras proceeded to extend the reach of his heptachord to an octachord, he did not violate this law—as had been done by other musicians.[6] On the contrary, he maintained the fundamental structure of both tetrachords in his scale by the simple, but musically innovative, expedient of intercalating a whole-tone between them. As Nicomachus makes clear, Pythagoras' motivation in this effort was essentially musical. Above all, it was informed by and derived from Pythagoras' musical intelligence. To begin with, Pythagoras knew that in his heptachord consisting of two conjunct tetrachords, the basic distribution of intervals had to be maintained for all melodic purposes. This required that each note of the heptachord be distant by the interval of a fourth from the fourth note in succession from it.[7] Given the heptachord, therefore, the successive notes would stand in the following relations:

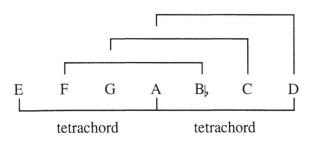

E F G A B♭ C D

tetrachord   tetrachord

This principle of melodic succession is thus controlled in the following transferences, in which, as Nicomachus explains, the semi-tones between E and F and A and B♭ by virtue of their distinctive positions, serve a real melodic purpose:[8]

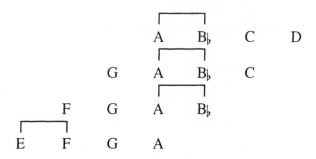

Indeed, as is evident, none of the above transferences would be possible were not the original form of the tetrachord maintained. And the same thing holds true for the octachord; for maintaining the basic form of the tetrachord in this case requires a new distribution of intervals, one in which two semi-tones figure prominently in the various transferences detailed by Nicomachus. As he says, therefore, it makes no difference whether one construes the octachord as a tetrachord and a pentachord in conjunction with one another or as two tetrachords in disjunction from one another; in either case the same progression results: each note of the octachord is distant by the interval of a fifth from the fifth note succeeding it. Given the octachord, then, the successsive notes would stand in the following relations:

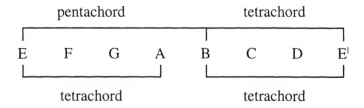

In the following inversions the semi-tones therefore occupy these positions:

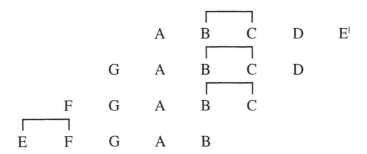

This purely musical analysis demonstrates that in the ancient heptachord there are two melodically vital semi-tones: E–F and A–B♭. Similarly, in the Dorian octachord there are also two semi-tones, one identical to that of the heptachord: E–F, the other no less melodically significant: B–C. Most important, these semi-tones are dictated by the natural laws of melodic consecution, and so firmly rooted were those laws in Pythagoras' musical intelligence that throughout the course of his musical innovations he did not allow himself to transgress them.[9]

To a musician, configurations and their inversions such as the ones represented above are not mere theoretical abstractions. They are representations of real melodic possibilities, their various permutations each carrying modal implications of great melodic import.[10] In Pythagoras' octachord, for example, the potential for melody is almost incalculable: within its confines lie all the elements for the great and memorable melodies composed from antiquity down to the present day. The opening theme from Mozart's *Sonata in C Major* K545, for example, is composed of the same elements as those detailed by Nicomachus in this chapter. Thus, implicit in Pythagoras' octachord are these melodic items:

$$E \quad F \quad G \quad A \quad C$$

which, instantiated in Mozart's pitch range, become

$$B \quad C \quad D \quad E \quad G$$

And they are brought to life by Mozart in the celebrated theme:

Contemplating such a melody, an ancient musician would have noticed that the semi-tone (B–C), an integral part of the theme, is in the first position (as in Nicomachus' inversion on p. 103 above).[11] And it is in fact given special emphasis by Mozart through a strong rhythmic pause—a thesis—on the dotted quarter note (B).[12] Most importantly, without access to that semi-tone, Mozart could not have composed his melody (nor, for that matter, could the eminent composers of antiquity have composed those melodies for which they too were once celebrated). As Nicomachus shows in his various inversions, therefore, the semi-tone was very much a feature of musical life. But there was something peculiar about it, something discomfiting to Nicomachus, a fact which he evinces in the phrase "the semi-tone so-called." Something was indeed wrong with the semi-tone, and Pythagoras discovered what it was the moment he applied his mathematical principles to determine the positions of the interior notes of the tetrachord in the three genera.[13]

Notes to Chapter 7

1. This entire chapter is copied by Iamblichus, *De vita pyth*, 120–121 (Deubner, 69.5–70. 2). See Guthrie (1988), pp. 86–87.
2. See above, Chapter 6, pp. 91–92. Cf. D. R. Fideler in Guthrie (1988), p. 27 where these relations are presented in a diagram that is correlated with the piano keyboard (Figure 7).
3. *Od.* 5.63ff.
4. In his *Intro. Arithm.* 2.8.3 (Hoche, 91.10), Nicomachus uses the word φυσικός in the Aristotelian sense of "natural." In this case, he is concerned to deal with numbers that combine in certain "natural" series, i.e., series that are natural to the science of arithmetic. Here, however, he is concerned with certain series or progressions that are natural not to the science of arithmetic, but solely and peculiarly to the art of music. As if to emphasize this point, he almost exhausts the lexicon of words meaning "progression:" βαθμός, πρόδος, μετάβασις, προχώρησις, προβάδην, μεταβαίνω. It is the same stylistic device he used in Chapter 6 to emphasize the factor, weight (above, p. 91).
5. This progression is understood by Aristoxenus as embodying the principle of the diatonic genus (*Harm. El.* 1.23; Da Rios, 29.10–11). According to this principle, every generic division of the tetrachord, whether it be the chromatic (semi-tone, semi-tone, tone and a half) or the enharmonic (quarter-tone, quarter-tone, ditone), must not exceed or fall short of the succession: semi-tone, whole-tone, whole-tone. This is one of music's underived rules. It cannot be demonstrated from any higher principle but must be grasped solely by the musically cognizant ear. See Barker, II, (1989), p. 141, n. 88.
6. See above, Chapter 5, pp. 77–78.
7. This second and most indispensable principle is stated by Aristoxenus, *Harm. El.* 2.54 (Da Rios, 67.6–8): "Let it be accepted that in every genus, as the melodic sequence progresses through successive notes both up and down from any given note, it must make with the fourth successive note the concord of a fourth or with the fifth successive note the concord of a fifth" (trans. Barker). The concords of fifths are achieved with Pythagoras' Dorian octachord. As Barker, II, (1989), p. 146, n. 124, explains, these principles depend on the assumption that any scale or extended *systema* is analyzable into

similar tetrachords arranged by conjunction or disjunction.

8. These transferences are termed by the theorists species (*eide*) or *schemata*. As is explained by Barker, II, (1989), p. 127, n. 7, "One structure differs in *schema* from another of equal magnitude if their constituent intervals are the same in size and number, but are differently ordered."

9. On the basis of these musical progressions, the Aristoxenians always maintained with unwavering conviction that the octave consists of five equal whole-tones and two equal semi-tones. See Levin (1975), p. 29, n. 33.

10. In the most general sense of the word, mode denotes a selection of notes that are arranged in a certain predetermined order and that can be realized in any pitch range desired. Taken in the aggregate, these notes so arranged constitute the basic tonal substance of a musical composition. Although the Greeks firmly believed that the character or *ethos* of a melody depended primarily on the mode in which it was composed, scholars to this day differ on the particular forms these Greek modes took to produce their effects on the listener. For a general discussion, see Anderson, pp. 25–33.

11. To an ancient musician, the semi-tone in this position would be recognizable for embodying a fundamental characteristic of the Lydian mode, i.e., that mode which matches most closely the modern scale of C Major.

12. The rhythmic pause is on that metrical segment which the ancients called the "downbeat" or *thesis*. The "upbeat" was termed *arsis*.

13. Although Nicomachus hints at the problem with the semi-tone in the next two chapters, it is not until the final chapter that he states what it is when he asks (p. 175): "If these semi-tones were really halves of whole-tones, what would prevent a whole-tone from being composed of them . . . ?" But he was obviously so reluctant to broach this truly catastrophic development with regard to the semi-tone that he postpones the subject to some future occasion. It is not until *Excerpt* 2 (pp. 189–90) that we find Nicomachus straining at every mathematical method possible to resolve the difficulty: the whole tone cannot be divided into two equal parts.

Chapter 8

Explanation of the references
to harmonics in the *Timaeus*

IT IS USEFUL, now that we have reached this point, to open up at this opportune moment the passage in the *Psychogony* in which Plato expressed himself as follows: "so that within each interval there are two means, the one superior and inferior to the extremes by the same fraction, the other by the same number. He (the Demiurge) filled up the distance between the hemiolic interval [3:2] and the epitritic [4:3] with the remaining interval of the sesquioctave [9:8]."

For the double interval is as 12 is to 6, but there are two means, 9 and 8. The number 8, however, in the harmonic proportion is midway between 6 and 12, being greater than 6 by one third of 6 (that is, 2), and being less than 12 by one third of 12 (that is, 4). That is why Plato said that the mean, 8, inasmuch as it is of the harmonic proportion, is greater and lesser than the extremes by the same fraction. For the greatest term compared with the smallest is thus in a double proportion; and so it follows that the difference between the greatest term and the middle is 4, compared with the difference between the middle and the smallest, which is 2; for these differences are in a double proportion, 4 to 2. The peculiar property of such a mean is that, when the extremes are added to one another and multiplied by the middle term, a product is yielded which is the double of the product of the extremes; for 8 multiplied by the sum of the extremes, that is, 18, gives 144, which is double the product of the extremes, that is, 72.

The other mean, 9, which is fixed at the paramese degree, is observed to be at the arithmetic mean between the extremes, being less than 12 and greater than 6 by the same number (3). And the peculiar property of this mean is that the sum of the extremes is the double of the middle term itself, and the square of the middle term (which is 81) is greater than the product of the extremes (that is, 72) by the whole square of the differences, that is, by 3 times 3, or 9, for this is the difference.

One can also point out the third mean, more properly called "proportion," in both the middle terms, 9 and 8. For 12 is in the same proportion to 8 as 9 is to 6; for both are in a hemiolic proportion. And the product of the extremes is equal to the product of the middle terms, 12 times 6 being equal to 9 times 8.

Commentary 8

THE ELABORATION of the musical progressions and inversions which Nicomachus presents in Chapter 7 embodies a critical implication for harmonic science, namely, that Pythagoras had succeeded in doing for the musical intervals smaller than a whole-tone what he had done for the consonances and the whole-tone, that is, define their magnitudes in mathematically rational terms. This is tantamount to suggesting that Pythagoras had succeeded in defining mathematically the positions of all the interior notes of the tetrachord—those notes called "movable," or *kinoumenoi*, by the musical theorists—and that he had accomplished this for all three genera.[1] Nicomachus' implicit claims for Pythagoras are therefore quite far-reaching. The problem is, however, that nowhere does he provide any mathematical evidence to support these claims.[2] Instead, he simply details in Chapter 7 what Pythagoras knew to be true a priori about the progression of the movable notes in one of the genera—the diatonic. By applying this knowledge to the heptachord as well as the octachord, Pythagoras, as Nicomachus then proceeded to explain, could then anticipate exactly where the semi-tone would appear in each species of the tetrachords.

Given the detail in which Nicomachus describes Pythagoras' understanding of the musical function of the semi-tone and of the important role it plays in the tetrachordal inversions, the reader might reasonably expect that Nicomachus would commence Chapter 8 with Pythagoras' mathematical determination of the semitone. But this was clearly not meant to be; for at this critical juncture Nicomachus engages in an openly diversionary tactic: instead of dealing with the semi-tone and the problems it poses for mathematical regimentation, Nicomachus leads the reader away from this highly problematic area and directs her attention instead to the mathematically elegant structures that Plato set out in the *Timaeus*.

In providing the mathematical basis for the musical concords, Pythagoras had made a fundamental contribution to the mathematization of music. As Nicomachus had explained earlier in Chapter

6, Pythagoras proved that the exterior notes of the tetrachord—those notes termed "fixed" (*hestotes*) by the musical theorists—were mathematically expressible in the epitritic ratio 4:3. In like manner, he had worked out the ratios for the other concords.

As it happens, the notes expressed by these ratios were also understood as "fixed" by the musical theorists. For them, however, they were fixed not in any mathematical sense but, rather, by the laws of musical logic. According to these laws, the notes bounding the limits of the tetrachord remain fixed or unchanged in pitch in all the extended scales, whether these scales were formed by conjunction, as in the heptachord, or by disjunction, as in the octachord.[3] Considered in the purely abstract terms of musical logic—that is, with reference not to actual pitches but only to pitch relations—the heptachord comprises two tetrachords bounded by the fixed notes hypate (E)–mese (A) and by mese (A)–nete (D) that are conjoined on the note mese:

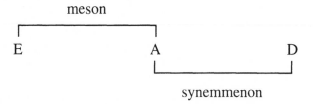

The lower tetrachord came to be called *meson*, literally, tetrachord of the middle notes; the upper tetrachord was named after its function, *synemmenon*, tetrachord of the "conjunct notes."

Taken in the same abstract terms, the octachord is seen to comprise two tetrachords which are bounded by the fixed notes hypate (E)–mese (A) and paramese (B)–the Dorian nete, so-called (E'), the two tetrachords separated by the disjunctive whole-tone between mese (A) and paramese (B):

The lower tetrachord, *meson*, is distant by a whole-tone from the upper tetrachord, which came to be called *diezeugmenon*, the tetrachord of the "disjunct notes." The new relations entailed by the octachord thus comprise the fifth between the notes hypate (E) and paramese (B) as well as between mese (A) and the new nete (E'), the nete of the *diezeugmenon* tetrachord. These relations were found by Pythagoras to be expressed in the ratio 3:2. And the combined fourth and fifth he proved mathematically to be equal to an octave.

These relations once having been established by musical logic, it is a simple matter to translate them into the concrete terms of actual pitches. Selecting any pitch arbitrarily and requiring it to function as any one of the fixed pitches described above, one can reconstruct from that function all the other pitches in their fixed relations to that initial pitch. Given the heptachord then, let B♭ function as mese; F will be hypate, and E♭ will be nete synemmenon:

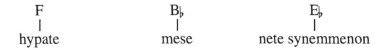

Again, let the pitch G function as hypate; C will be mese, and F will be nete synemmenon:

Finally, let C♯ function as nete synemmenon; D♯ will be hypate, and G♯ will be mese:

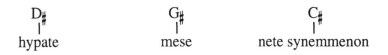

The same musically logical laws hold true for the fixed notes of the octachord. Thus, for example, let F be mese; G will be paramese, C will be hypate, and C^l will be nete diezeugmenon:

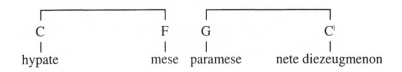

Again, let C be paramese; mese will be B♭, hypate will be F, and nete diezeugmenon will be F^l:

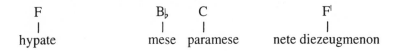

Finally, let D function as hypate; D^l will be nete diezeugmenon, G will be mese, and A will be paramese:

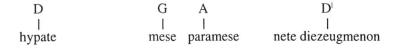

All musical functions such as these are thus "fixed" by the laws of musical logic, and the actual pitches of music must reflect these logically ordained functions.

When, therefore, Pythagoras found a way to express these musical relations in mathematical terms, he constructed a utopian ideal, a totally enclosed and self-contained cosmos in which all the parts fit together to form a perfect unity.[4] Rooted as it was in mathematical truth, that unity was rendered explicit, coherent, knowable, and absolute. And it was never to be confuted by the senses. This was the moment of truth at which Nicomachus arrived in Chapter 7. It was the critical moment when the abstract laws of musical theory coincided with those of mathematics, when the concurrency of these laws in the concrete musical pitches of fourths, fifths, and octaves gave rise to sensible objects of a particularized beauty. At this moment the seeker of wisdom was given the means to discriminate between the appearance of beauty in particular and the unconditional reality of beauty in general. The appearance of beauty lay in the particular consonances—fourths, fifths, and octaves—however various the actual pitches they inhabited; but the unconditional reality of their beauty resided in the absolute, immutable, and eternal laws to which they owed their allegiance. Their appearance was given to the ear to apprehend, but their reality could be communicated only to the mind and, hence, could be assumed to qualify as a true object of knowledge.

To direct his reader to the reality of that beauty expressed by the mathematical laws of concordancy, Nicomachus could not do better than refer her to the *Timaeus* of Plato. For in that work Plato gave new meaning to the Pythagorean super-sensible harmonic universe by enclosing it within the mathematically fixed limits of four octaves and a major sixth. But most importantly, he succeeded in doing this without enlisting the help of empirical tests of any sort and without having recourse to any a priori musical knowledge. His method was purely mathematical. The passage in the *Timaeus* to which Nicomachus refers his reader's attention is identified by him as the *Psychogonia*, or Generation of the Soul.[5] The soul in this case is of course that of the cosmos, and the passage in question is that of *Tim.* 35A–36D7.

The quotation from the *Psychogonia* with which Nicomachus begins Chapter 8 comes from Plato's discussion concerning the creation of the World-Soul by the Demiurge (the Master-Craftsman), from the disparate ingredients Sameness, Otherness, and Being: "Taking these three ingredients together, the Demiurge blended them all into a single form, forcing Otherness to come into tune with Sameness despite its unwillingness to mingle. Mixing them with Being, the Demiurge made from the three a unity and next proceeded to divide this whole into as many parts as was suitable."[6] These parts, as Plato goes on to explain, were determined by the numbers forming two geometrical progressions of which the last term is the twenty-seventh multiple of the first term, or:

$$27 = 1 + 2 + 3 + 4 + 8 + 9$$

And, as Plutarch informs us, it was already traditional in his day to represent these two progressions by a diagram in the shape of a Lambda,[7] on one side of which are Plato's duple intervals, on the other, his triple intervals:

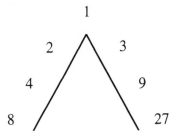

Having reached this point in his description of the Demiurge's progress, Plato goes on to say:

> After this, he [the Demiurge] proceeded to fill up both the duple and the triple intervals, cutting off still more parts from thence and inserting them between these terms (and here begins Nicomachus' quotation), "so that within each interval there are two means, the one superior and inferior to the extremes by the same fraction, the other by the same number."[8]

Nicomachus' rendering of the following passage in Plato is therefore misleadingly abridged:

> And when from these links there were generated the hemiolic [3:2] and epitritic [4:3] and sesquioctave [9:8] intervals within the original intervals, he proceeded to fill up all the epitritic intervals with the sesquioctave interval leaving over a fraction from each

of them, this remaining interval of the fraction having the numerical terms of 256 to 243.[9]

What Nicomachus has excised from Plato's passage is the computation of the interval called *leimma*, literally, the "remaining" interval, or semi–tone, after the insertion of the whole-tones, or sesquioctave intervals, in the fourth. Thus Nicomachus:

> He [the Demiurge] filled up the distance between the hemiolic interval and the epitritic with the remaining interval of the sesquioctave.

As Nicomachus has it, then, the dimensions of the octave, fourth, fifth, and whole-tone, which Pythagoras discovered through his empirical tests on strings of various lengths, were now corroborated by Plato through various operations of a purely mathematical nature. These operations consisted in Plato's construction of the two geometric progressions in which the ratios betwen the terms is 2:1 and 3:1, respectively:[10]

$$1\ 2\ 4\ 8 \text{ and } 1\ 3\ 9\ 27$$

Combining these two progressions, Plato produced the seventermed series:

$$1\ 2\ 3\ 4\ 8\ 9\ 27$$

The numbers in this series thus embody the ratios productive of the octave (2:1), the octave and a fifth (3:1), the double octave (4:1), the triple octave (8:1), the fifth (3:2), the fourth (4:3), and the whole-tone (9:8). The entire compass from one to the twenty-seventh multiple comprises therefore four octaves and a major sixth. Put into numerical terms, four octaves, or 16:1, plus a fifth (3:2), plus a whole-tone (9:8), equals 27:1, or:

$$16{:}1 \times 3{:}2 \times 9{:}8 = 27{:}1$$

This can be represented in musical notation as follows:

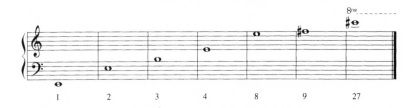

1   2   3   4   8   9   27

According to Nicomachus, Plato, having determined the limits of his cosmic attunement, proceeded first to locate in each of the octaves the harmonic mean—that mean which is superior and inferior to the extremes by the same fraction. Expressing this operation algebraically, Plato found the harmonic mean b in the series $a\ b\ c$, by applying the operation:[11]

$$b = \frac{2ac}{a+c}$$

Accordingly, Plato determined the interval of a fourth or, as Nicomachus explains, he established the harmonic mean in the ratio 12:6, this mean being superior to 6 by the same fraction as it is inferior to 12, or:

$$12{:}8 = 8{:}6$$

The ratio expressing this relationship is that of the fourth, or 4:3.

Next, Plato proceeds to locate in each of the octaves the arithmetic mean—that mean which is, as Nicomachus says, superior and inferior to the extremes by the same number.[12] In algebraic terms, Plato found the arithmetic mean b in the series $a\ b\ c$ by applying the operation:

$$b = \frac{a+c}{2}$$

In that way, Plato determined the interval of a fifth or, as Nicomachus explains, he established the arithmetic mean in the ratio 12:6, this being superior and inferior to the extremes by the same number (=3):

$$12:9 = 9:6$$

This means that Plato, by inserting the harmonic and arithmetic means respectively between each of the terms in the two geometric progressions—1, 2, 4, 8 and 1, 3, 9, 27—succeeded in corroborating mathematically everything that Pythagoras had discovered on the strings of his lyre. To begin with, Plato located the interval of a fourth by computing the harmonic mean between the terms 1 and 2, representative of the octave:

Let $a = 1$ and $c = 2$

$$b = \frac{2ac}{a+c}$$

$$b = \frac{2 \times 2}{3}$$

$$b = \frac{4}{3}$$

and this is representative of the notes:

E	A	E$^|$
1	$\frac{4}{3}$	2

Next, Plato located the arithmetic mean which fixes the note B, or paramese, between the octave limits E–E$^|$, that mean which is equal to half the sum of the extremes:

$$b = \frac{a+c}{2} \quad \text{or} \quad a+c = 2b$$

Let $a = 1$ and $c = 2$

$$b = \frac{1+2}{2}$$

$$b = \frac{3}{2}$$

Therefore,

$$1 \qquad \frac{3}{2} \qquad 2$$

and this is representative of the notes:

E	B	E$^{|}$
1	$\frac{3}{2}$	2

Plato thus determined the following means:

harmonic		arithmetic	
	|	|	
E	A	B	E$^{|}$
	|	|	
1	$\frac{4}{3}$	$\frac{3}{2}$	2

Putting all this together in his two geometric series, Plato obtained the following:

(1)	4/3	3/2	(2)	8/3	3	(4)	16/3	6	(8)
(1)	3/2	2	(3)	9/2	6	(9)	27/2	18	(27)

Combining the two series, Plato obtained:

(1) 4/3 3/2 (2) 8/3 (3) (4) 9/2 16/3 6 (8) (9) 27/2 18 (27)

Taking the first four terms in parentheses—1, 2, 3, 4—which yield two octaves, the following pitches are established:[13]

1	4/3	3/2	2	8/3	3	4
E	A	B	E^I	A^I	B^I	E^{II}

Having reached this stage in setting out Plato's computations, Nicomachus ends Chapter 8, thus leaving his reader with the impression that Plato had succeeded merely in rendering mathematically what Pythagoras had formulated from his experiments with musical instruments.[14] But, as is evident from the portion of the *Timaeus* which Nicomachus failed to quote, Plato went far beyond what Nicomachus has represented. For Plato succeeded in doing what had never been done before, not even by Pythagoras himself: he filled up all the intervals of a fourth with whole-tones, leaving over in each a remaining fraction, or *leimma*. In other words, Plato completed all the degrees in a diatonic scale:[15]

1	9/8	81/64	4/3	3/2	27/16	243/128	2
E	F♯	G♯	A	B	C♯	D♯	E^I

In so doing, Plato demonstrated that the fraction remaining in the fourth after the insertion of the two whole-tones is the semi-tone (as between G♯ and A; between D♯ and E♭):

$$\frac{4}{3} \div \left(\frac{9}{8} \times \frac{9}{8}\right) \text{ or } \frac{4}{3} \div \frac{81}{64} = \frac{256}{243}$$

Or, to put it another way, the semi-tone was shown by Plato to be anything but the half of a whole-tone. The semi-tone that is left over in the diatonic tetrachord when two whole-tones are subtracted from the fourth equals the so-called *leimma* (256:243). This is somewhat smaller than the semi-tone computed by dividing the whole-tone in half or:

$$\sqrt{9:8} = 3:2\sqrt{2}$$

Thus, Plato's calculations led to the inescapable fact that there was no center to the octave, no halving of the whole-tone, no perfect union of opposites, no rationality to the cosmos. This was a shattering development for the Pythagoreans, and it had to be hidden from view.[16] In this critical endeavor, Nicomachus did his part by misrepresenting Plato and putting off to some future time consideration of the dreaded subject.

Notes to Chapter 8

1. As Nicomachus explains in Chapter 8, the notes intervening between the limits of the tetrachord form three intervals of varying size depending upon the genus of the tetrachord. Because these interior notes shift position according to the laws of generic distribution, the theorists thought of them as "movable."

2. It would appear that before the time of Plato no attempt had been made to divide the tetrachord into parts mathematically. According to Ptolemy, *Harm*. 1.13 (Düring, 30.9ff.), Archytas, the fourth century B.C.E. countryman of Philolaus, was the first Pythagorean to determine the sizes of the intervals in the three genera. Cf. Taylor, p. 139.

3. The "fixed" notes are those that "stand still" (*hestotes*) despite any change in the genus of the tetrachord. These notes are the extremes of the tetrachord. They were called "immovable" (*akinetoi*) by Aristoxenus, *Harm. El*. 1.22 (Da Rios, 28.11).

4. According to Diogenes Laertius 8.48, Pythagoras was the first to speak of the heavens (*ouranos*) as a *cosmos*, literally, a "well-ordered" construction, in the sense of a whole complex of sun, moon, planets, and earth perfectly arranged. As such, it came to be thought of as a "universe." Cf. Taylor, pp. 65–66.

5. The passage in Plato's *Timaeus* to which Nicomachus applies this name—*Psychogonia*—is the subject of a commentary by Plutarch entitled *On the Generation of the Soul in the Timaeus*. The term *Psychogonia* seems not to have been used in this connection before the time of Plutarch and Nicomachus.

6. See *Excerpt* 7 (Jan, 278.10ff.), p. 195 where Nicomachus speaks of this tripartite composition of the soul as a discovery of Pythagoras.

7. On the *Lambda* pattern, see Plutarch *On the Generation of the Soul in the Timaeus* or, as it is commonly cited, *De gen. anima* 1017 (Cherniss, 273). See also, Brumbaugh, p. 227; McClain, p. 63, who continues to infinity all the integer products of 2 and 3 in "continued geometric progressions" of 1:2, 2:3, and 1:3. Cf. Fig. 23 on p. 65.

8. *Tim*. 35A6–B2.

9. *Tim*. 36A6–B5.

10. Cf. Levin (1975), p. 89.

11. As Nicomachus points out in his *Intro. Arithm.* 2.25.2 (Hoche, 132.11ff.), among the peculiar properties of the harmonic proportion is the fact that the ratio of the greatest term to the middle is greater than that of the middle to the smallest term. In terms of musical theory, this means that the fourth (determined mathematically to be at the harmonic mean between the extremes of the octave) is proven to be smaller than the fifth or: 12:8>8:6. It is this property that made the harmonic proportion appear contrary to the arithmetic. On the harmonic mean and its mathematical relation to the arithmetic mean, see Brumbaugh, pp. 217–18.

12. As Nicomachus points out in his *Intro. Arithm.* 2.23.1 (Hoche, 124.1ff.), the essential property which defines an arithmetic series is the equality of the differences between its successive terms. That being the case, 12:9<9:6. And this proves that the interval of a fifth, determined to be at the arithmetic mean between the extremes of the octave, is greater than the fourth.

13. The combination of the harmonic with the arithmetic gives what Nicomachus called in his *Intro. Arithm.* 2.29.1 (Hoche, 144.20–23) the "most perfect" proportion, since it embraces all three proportions (harmonic, arithmetic, and geometric) and is therefore "most useful for all progress in music and in the study of the nature of the universe."

14. The third mean with which Nicomachus ends the chapter is the geometric. In this type of proportion, it is no longer a question of the absolute differences between the middle term and each of the extremes, but the relative differences. That is, in the geometric proportion, *a* must be to *b* as *b* is to *c*.

15. The total compass of Plato's "Timaeus" scale is far greater than any scale system employed by the ancient Greeks either theoretically or practically. Commenting on this fact, Adrastus *apud* Theon (Hiller, 64.1ff.) notes that Aristoxenus treated of no attunement more extended than two octaves and a fourth, the limit of the Greater Perfect System, that system which contains the different modes of which musicians availed themselves. But, as Adrastus pointed out, Plato's construction was not intended to be sung or even heard by the human ear. It was for all intents and purposes, an "unheard" construction. Interestingly enough, however, that octave which was "filled up" by

NOTES TO CHAPTER EIGHT   123

the Demiurge corresponds in its disposition of intervals to the modal segment of the Greater Perfect System known as the Lydian scale. 16. On the mathematical determination of the *leimma*, see R. and D. Lawlor, pp. 43–46. According to one story, Hippasus, a disciple of Pythagoras, was expelled from the society of Pythagoreans for revealing this irrationality of the semi-tone, while another account had him drowned at sea for this misdemeanor. Cf. Taylor, p. 141. See, also, Levin (1975), p. 6, n. 9.

Chapter 9

The evidence of Philolaus concerning our statements

THAT the ancients also offered explanations that are in agreement with what has been demonstrated by us—on the one hand, calling the octave *harmonia*, and the fourth *syllaba* (for it is the first "taking together" of consonant notes), and the fifth *dioxeian* (for the fifth, progressing towards the treble, is adjacent to the primitive consonance, the fourth), and, on the other hand, asserting that the system formed of both intervals, the *syllaba* and the *dioxeian*, is the octave (called *harmonia* from the very fact that it is the first consonance "fitted together" from consonant intervals)—Philolaus, the successor of Pythagoras, makes evident by speaking to this effect in the first book of his *On Nature*. Because of haste, we shall content ourselves with a single witness even though many others have often made similar statements on the same subject. The text of Philolaus reads as follows:

> The size of a *harmonia* is a *syllaba* and a *dioxeian*. The *dioxeian* is greater than the *syllaba* by a sesquioctave. For from *hypata* to *mesa* is a *syllaba*, and from *mesa* to *neata*, a *dioxeian*; from *neata* to *trita* is a *syllaba*, and from *trita* to *hypata*, a *dioxeian*. The interval between *trita* and *mesa* is a sesquioctave, the *syllaba* is epitritic, the *dioxeian* is *hamiolic* and the *dia pasan* is a double proportion. Thus a *harmonia* consists of five sesquioctaves and two *dieseis*. A *dioxeian* is three sesquioctaves and a *diesis*, a *syllaba* is two sesquioctaves and a *diesis*.

We must remember that Philolaus means by trite, the note in the heptachord, now called paramese, but called trite before the insertion of the disjunctive whole-tone in the octachord. For this note was distant from paraneate by an incomposite trihemitone, from which interval the intercalated string subtracted a whole-tone, and the remaining semi-tone between trite and paramese was left in the disjunction. Consequently, the ancient trite was distant from the nete by a fourth, which interval the paramese has now assumed in its stead. But there are those who do not understand this and claim that it is impossible for trite to be distant from nete by an interval in the epitritic proportion. Others say not unpersuasively that the intercalated note was not inserted between mese and trite, but between trite and paraneate; but that the ancient trite became paramese in the disjunction; and that Philolaus calls the paramese by the former name, trite, although it was distant from the nete by a fourth.

Commentary 9

THE GREATEST discovery of Pythagoras and his disciples consisted in the principle about the musical consonances, that the pitch produced by a plucked string depends upon the length of the string and that strings whose lengths are to each other as the ratio of whole numbers produce the consonances: fourths, fifths, and octaves.[1] Unfortunately, this principle led to the most troublesome, deep-seatedly refractory, number in all of Pythagorean harmonics: the square root of 2. It was a troublesome number because it could not be expressed as a ratio of whole numbers. And that meant that it could not be added to nor subtracted from whole numbers; neither could it divide nor be divided by them. In short, it was a number that would not participate on any rational basis with the other numbers in the range of harmonic science. Yet, as Nicomachus, in spite of himself, demonstrated in Chapter 3, it was implicitly involved—as a semi-tone—in the heptachordal structure of the cosmos. It was understandably then a horror to the Pythagoreans since, in its lack of integrity and its irrationality, it was a number that threatened to undermine their whole philosophy of universal harmony.[2]

Plato had come upon this number independently of the Pythagoreans when, in the *Timaeus* passage quoted above (pp. 114–15), he had the Demiurge fill up the fourth—the limits of the tetrachord—in the proportion 4:3, i.e with two whole-tones. But, as the Demiurge discovered, two whole-tones do not completely fill up the fourth; something is left over, and this something, according to musical logic, is a semi-tone. From the standpoint of mathematical logic, however, it is a kind of *teras*, a freak of musical nature—not quite a semi-tone, but something less than the half of a whole-tone. It is a residue, or "remainder" (λεῖμμα), that is inexpressible by any rational means. Plato computed it as 256:243, since this is what is left over when two whole-tones are subtracted from the fourth:

$$4 : 3 \div (9 : 8 \times 9 : 8) \;=\; 4 : 3 \div 81 : 64 \;=\; 256 : 243$$

And this ungainly ratio is what represents a small semi-tone, i.e. an interval that is something less than a true half of a whole-tone. In omitting to mention the critical step by which Plato arrived at this ratio, Nicomachus in Chapter 8 accomplished two things: first, he left the impression in the mind of his reader that Plato had merely corroborated Pythagoras' determination of the consonances, whereas Plato had in fact not only determined the interior intervals of the fourth but had also approximated the value of the semi-tone[3] and, second, Nicomachus diverted his reader's attention from the problem of the semi-tone, a fact of musical life with which musicians must grapple to this very day.[4]

In the first half of the present chapter, we find Nicomachus proceeding along much the same lines as earlier, focusing on the same material—the consonances—and quite skillfully diverting his reader from the question of the semi-tone. But the overwrought opening sentence of this chapter betrays a certain discomfiture on his part, one phrase being interrupted by another with parenthetical commentary, the complex whole barely held in syntactical check by the slackened reins of the word "that" (ὅτι). That this device serves to delay the appearance of the sentence subject— Philolaus—suggests a certain deference on Nicomachus' part to the celebrity of this great Pythagorean savant; but whatever the case, by proceeding in this fashion, Nicomachus succeeds quite well in achieving his primary goal: to postpone discussion of the problematic semi-tone. The question of the dreaded semi-tone aside, however, Nicomachus did perform a major service to the history of Pythagorean thought by quoting from a work of Philolaus, the first Pythagorean to have committed any of the precepts of Pythagoras to writing.[5] And since most of Philolaus' writings are irrecoverably lost to us, the transmission of any fragment by a scholar such as Nicomachus is of incalculable worth.

Philolaus came from Tarentum in southern Italy, a celebrated Pythagorean center, and lived sometime in the last decades of the fifth century B.C.E. Born too late, therefore, to have heard for himself the words of the Master, he nonetheless can be thought of as having written down with scrupulous care whatever he heard from the lips of Pythagoras' successors. So that when he wrote, for example, "All the things which can be known have number; for it is not possible that we can conceive anything or know anything without number," it is as though we are hearing the words of Pythagoras himself.[6] Before Philolaus, no one, it seems, had ever dreamt of writing down anything that Pythagoras said. Indeed, to perform such an act would have been to violate the tabu established by the Master himself. For in the society that Pythagoras founded, all scientific and mathematical discoveries were considered collective property and, in some mystical sense, regarded as oblations to Pythagoras himself, this convention being observed even after his death. Whether Pythagoras and his disciples bound themselves to this rule by a pledge of secrecy, or whether they simply put a greater value on the unseen medium of the spoken word, has long been debated by scholars; but one thing is certain: there is no trace of any Pythagorean written record before Philolaus.

To Nicomachus, therefore, Philolaus was a "most ancient" witness, one of the venerated παλαιότατοι and, as characterized by Nicomachus, a direct successor, or διάδοχος, of Pythagoras himself. This is in fact to exaggerate the antiquity of Philolaus, since he was actually a contemporary of Socrates. In any case, however, Philolaus was the earliest Pythagorean, and in that sense the "most ancient," to have published anything at all on Pythagorean doctrine. The work from which Nicomachus derived his quotation was, apparently, a multi-volume treatise entitled *On Nature*. It opened with these words:

Nature in the cosmos is composed of a *harmonia* between the unlimited and the limited and so too is the whole cosmos and everything in it.[7]

The language of Philolaus is Doric, the Greek dialect spoken in the Peloponnese, in Dorian colonies on various Greek islands, and in Magna Graecia, that region in southern Italy where the Pythagoreans made Tarentum their great cultural and philosophical headquarters. It was there that the Pythagoreans also made Doric their lingua franca, so much so that in subsequent generations Pythagorean Doric came to be thought of as an Italiote Koine.[8]

It has long been believed that this Doric prose tradition began with Philolaus' countryman, Archytas, the friend of Plato who lived fully a generation after Philolaus. Assuming, however, that the fragments of Philolaus' writings are genuine, this scholarly opinion would need to be revised in Philolaus' favor.[9] In any case, the debate goes on.

Nicomachus' quotation from Philolaus, to judge it solely on linguistic grounds, appears to be altogether authentic, in that it adheres to all the norms of Pythagorean Doric. His quotation follows a passage from Philolaus' *On Nature* in which Philolaus explains what *harmonia* does:

> The essence of things, being eternal, and nature itself admit of divine and not of human knowledge; nor would it be possible for any of the things that exist and that are known by us to have come into being if the existence of the limited and the unlimited, of which the cosmos is composed, were not first assumed. But since these principles [i.e. opposites] are neither alike nor of the same race, it would now have been impossible for them to be brought into an ordered arrangement if *harmonia*, however it came into being, had not imposed itself upon them. Things that are alike and of the same race had no need of *harmonia*; but it was necessary for things that are dissimilar and not of the same race and not of equal standing to be locked together by *harmonia* so that they might be held together in a *cosmos* (literally, perfect arrangement).[10]

In the section from which Nicomachus is here quoting, Philolaus then proceeds to explain what *harmonia* is. And this, we learn, is an octave, or *dia pason*, literally, the interval which runs "through all the notes."

To prepare his reader for Philolaus' text, Nicomachus begins by defining each of the terms used by Philolaus: *syllaba*, the Doric form for Attic *syllabe*, denotes the interval of a fourth; *dioxeian*, Doric for Attic *dioxeion*, denotes the interval of a fifth; the "fitting together" or *harmonia* of the fourth and fifth is therefore the *dia pasan*, the Doric form for Attic *dia pason*, the interval which runs "through all the notes." Having defined Philolaus' terminology, Nicomachus then devotes the balance of the chapter to discussing how the octachord is formed, thus retracing much the same ground

as that of Chapter 5, with the difference only that here his explanation is even more tortuous than that in Chapter 5.

Quite apart from the problematic aspect of his octachord analysis, Nicomachus' discussion in this chapter—granted its interest
for the Philolaic terminology that it introduces—is especially
significant for what it omits. This is particularly the case as regards
the notion of *diesis*. The term occurs three times in the passage of
Philolaus quoted by Nicomachus—once in his analysis of the
octave as comprising five whole-tones and two *dieseis*, again in his
analysis of a fifth as comprising three whole-tones and two *dieseis*,
and finally in his analysis of the fourth as consisting of two whole-
tones and a *diesis*. From these uses it is clear that *diesis* can mean
only one thing: a semi-tone. But for Nicomachus to have mentioned *diesis*, to have defined it as he did *syllaba*, *dioxeian*, and
harmonia, would have entailed confrontation with the inharmoni-
ous semi-tone, something that he was obviously as reluctant to do
here as he was in Chapter 8, where he misquoted Plato to the same
purpose. So that here again Nicomachus forestalls any discussion
of irrationality, that most disagreeable property of the octave's
anatomy.

Philolaus' is the language of practicing musicians.[11] According to
Theophrastus, a student of Aristotle's, his terminology was also
consistently identified with the Pythagoreans:

> The Pythagoreans called the consonance of a fourth *syllabe*, that
> of the fifth *dioxeian*, and they determined that the octave was a
> *harmonia* of both.[12]

Accordingly, a Pythagorean musician, holding his tilted lyre,
would quite naturally be inclined to think of the first four strings
that fell conveniently to his left hand as a literal "grab" or, as
Philolaus has it, a *syllaba*. This is in fact confirmed by Aelian (170–
235 C.E.) who says:

> In lyre-type instrumental terms, it is called *syllabe* from the
> manner of the hand playing the lyre, since in the practice of the
> heptachord the first grab of the fingers was the consonance of the
> fourth.[13]

In contrast to *syllaba*, the colloquialism used by practicing musicians, *dia tettaron* is the term by which the musical theorists designated the fourth, or the interval that runs "through four notes."

Philolaus' term for the fifth is especially interesting for what it implies about the musicians' understanding of the octachord. Again, Aelian is instructive on this point:

> The fifth, because it is conjoined with the consonance of a fourth as one progresses upward in pitch, was called *dioxeian*, being composed of the higher-pitched notes of the octave.[14]

We know, of course, that in the Greeks' musical nomenclature the names of the individual notes of the scale were derived not from the pitch of the lyre strings, but rather from their position relative to the performer. Thus, the string lowest in position (nete) was the highest in pitch, while that in the highest position (hypate) was the lowest in pitch.[15] With the term *dioxeian*, however, we have direct evidence that the Greek musicians thought of the notes of the scale in ascending order, inasmuch as the term *dioxeian* equates the higher-pitched notes of the scale with the lyre strings in higher position.[16] Accordingly, as Aelian's evidence shows, a musician playing an eight-stringed lyre thought of the *dioxeian* in terms of those strings that succeed the first "grab," namely, those strings whose pitches run "through the high notes" of the octave. These notes of higher pitch would necessarily be the constituents of the upper fifth on the octachord, or that interval called by the theorists *dia pente*, the interval running "through five notes":

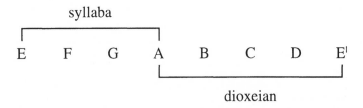

In sum then, Philolaus' statement about *harmonia* and its well-fitting components appears to be in total accord with the scale created by Pythagoras when he inserted a whole-tone in the heptachord. This alteration, as Nicomachus described it in Chapter 5, resulted in the rise in pitch of trite synemmenon (which he maintained the ancients had called paramese) to $B_{\natural}$, which came thereafter to be called paramese. Everything that Philolaus says in the statement quoted by Nicomachus appears, therefore, to comport easily with this Pythagorean octachord scale. As Nicomachus interprets this Philolaic evidence, however, a certain difficulty arises. The problem turns on the note called trite, a word which means "third note." As Nicomachus has it, before the insertion of the whole-tone in the heptachord, trite was in Philolaus' scale distant from paranete (D) by an interval of three semi-tones or, as Nicomachus calls it, a trihemitone. Moreover, Nicomachus says that this trihemitone was *asyntheton*, or incomposite. This means in Greek theory that the interval in question was not divided by the presence of any other note.[17] On Nicomachus' interpretation, therefore, Philolaus' scale was a defective heptachord in which trite— the ancient trite, as Nicomachus calls it—was distant from the octave note $E^|$ (nete) by a fourth, and at the same time incorporated a gap between B and D:[18]

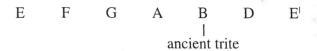

E   F   G   A   B   D   E^|
                    |
               ancient trite

When a new note was inserted into this heptachord, the ancient trite (B) came to be called paramese.

At this point Nicomachus suspects that his reader may be experiencing some confusion. He thus pauses to assure her that many others have been confused by these developments. This, he says, was because they could not envisage a scale in which trite was distant from nete by a fourth. His implication is that Philolaus' scale was by then so archaic that some theorists had lost all contact with it. Those who interpreted Philolaus' evidence to Nicomachus' apparent satisfaction maintained that a new note was inserted between Philolaus' trite (B) and his paramese (D). This note had to have been C, a note which, according to Nicomachus, subtracted a whole-tone (C–D) from the incomposite trihemitone (B–D):

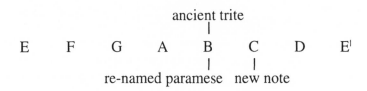

Nicomachus left untreated only one item: the *diesis*, Philolaus' term for the semi-tone.[19] As seems evident, Nicomachus considered this an inappropriate time to bring up so unruly a problem. This seems to me, however, as opportune a moment as any to examine the subject. Nicomachus, it will be remembered, did promise his reader a full explanation of this difficult problem at some later time. The fulfillment of this promise appears in *Excerpt* 2 which, as it happens, was a critical source for Boethius, who says:

> In truth, Philolaus, the Pythagorean, attempted to divide the whole-tone in another way, determining evidently that the origin of the whole-tone derived from that number which is the first to yield a cube from the first uneven number, a number especially esteemed by the Pythagoreans.[20]

This number, as Boethius goes on to explain, conceived by Philolaus to be the *primordium* of the whole-tone, was 27, the cube of 3, and a number highly esteemed by the Pythagoreans.[21] Significantly, this number emerges from the computations of Nicomachus in *Excerpt* 2 in the following fashion. The ratio of the fourth (4:3) is represented by the proportion 256:192. Starting from 192, if one adds to it the whole-tone ratio (9:8), the resulting number is 216. And 216:192 = 9:8. Again, the addition of another whole-tone, or 9:8, to 216 results in 243. And 243:216 = 9:8. The following sequence is established:

C   D   E   F
192 : 216 : 243 : 256

The peculiar property of these whole-tone ratios, 192:216 and 216:243, is that the difference between their terms, i.e. 24 and 27 respectively, is equal to the amount by which the one term exceeds the other in the ratio of 9:8. Or, as Nicomachus puts it, the sesquioctave of 192 is that number which contains 192 once and its eighth, or 24; and the same relation between the terms 216:243 yields the number 27, or an eighth of 216. As Boethius explains, 27, Philolaus' primordium, is to 24 as 9 is to 8. And the difference between 27 and 24 is the first uneven number (3) which, being an eighth of 24, yields when added to 24, the first cube of 3, or 27. Philolaus concentrated then on 27 and divided it into two parts, calling the lesser part of 13 units a *diesis*, and the greater part of 14 units, *apotome*. The difference between these parts (=1) he called *comma*, and a half of a *comma* he called *schisma*. This all means that Philolaus had calculated the *diesis* to be the difference between the terms of the *leimma* (256:243), or 13. Thus, when he computed the *harmonia* to be a complex of five whole-tones and two *dieseis*, Philolaus had in effect anticipated Plato's calculations in the *Timaeus*.

Division of the octave according to Plato, *Timaeus* 36A1–B5:

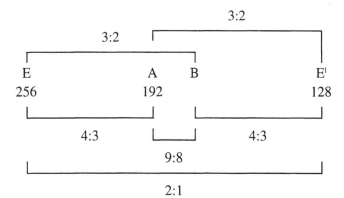

Division of the fourth according to Plato:

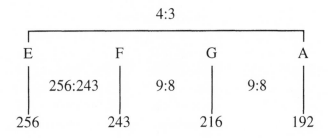

Division of the whole-tone according to Philolaus:[22]

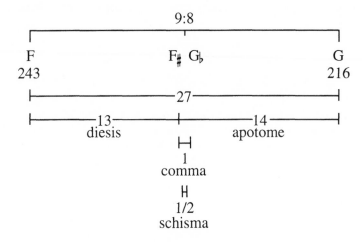

In the final analysis, it was to this that the Pythagoreans' harmonic analysis of the universe led: the discovery of incommensurables. And no matter how they might juxtapose the numbers, no matter to what lengths they might extend their mathematical circumlocutions, one fact remained, a fact that has ever since proved resistant to mathematical rationalization: there is no fraction m/n that will divide the whole-tone into two equal parts.

Notes to Chapter 9

1. Iamblichus lists the names of two hundred and eighteen disciples of Pythagoras arranged according to place of origin in *De vita Pyth.* 36.265–67 (Deubner, 142.10–146. 16). These, he says, were all well-known and celebrated for their promotion of the Master's teachings. Yet, he adds, the great majority of Pythagoras' learned disciples were anonymous, their names having long since fallen from memory. On the teachings of Pythagoras and the early Pythagoreans in the later doxographical tradition, see Thesleff (1961), pp. 117ff.

2. The discovery by Pythagoras and his immediate disciples that the sum of the squares on the sides forming a right angle is equal to the square on the remaining side—the hypotenuse—led, interestingly enough, to the same irrational number as that expressive of the semi-tone. For, if the hypotenuse is $x : x^2 = 1^2 + 1^2 = 2$. This means that the length of the hypotenuse must be a number whose square is 2 or $\sqrt{2}$. Thus, just as in the case of the whole-tone, there is no fraction m/n that will measure the hypotenuse of a right triangle. Problems such as these eventually led the Greek mathematicians to establish their geometry independently of arithmetic. For discussion, see Kline, pp. 36–39.

3. There is no trace of Plato's method for reaching this determination before the writing of the *Timaeus*, nor, for that matter, is there any trace of the *Timaeus* scale before his time. Cf. Taylor, pp. 139–40

4. This is a complex subject. The problem it raises can best be illustrated by the ancient Lydian mode (the scale of Plato's *Timaeus*) which, in Pythagorean intonation, bears a close resemblance to the modern major diatonic scale, but with these differences: the Pythagorean scale makes no distinction between major and minor whole-tones; its semi-tones are smaller than the modern diatonic semi-tones; its thirds (as between parhypate and mese or F and A) in the ratio 81:64 are sharper than the modern third. From antiquity to the present day, attempts have been made to reconcile the octave components with musical practices. To date, the most successful compromise with the octave's inherent irrationality is that pro-

vided by equal temperament. This involves the equalization of the twelve semi-tones in the octave. When this is accomplished, the frequency of each semi-tone is approximately 1.06 times the frequency of the one immediately below it. This causes the tempered fourth to be slightly sharp and the tempered fifth to be slightly flat. See Sir James Jeans, pp. 174ff.

5. See Heath (1913), p. 47.

6. *Vors.* 44B4. See Barker, II (1989), p. 36, 1.11.

7. *Vors.* 44Bl. See Barker, II (1989), p. 36, 1.9.

8. On the Doric dialect of the Pythagorean texts, see Thesleff (1961), pp. 91–93.

9. As Barker, II (1989), p. 36, n. 30 points out, many of the fragments that came down under the name Philolaus are spurious. He considers those having to do with *harmonia*, hence, the fragment quoted by Nicomachus, to be genuine. For arguments against the authenticity of these fragments, see Thesleff (1961), pp. 103–04.

10. *Vors.* 44B6. See Barker, II (1989), pp. 36–37, 1.12.

11. See Winnington-Ingram (1936), p. 56, n. 1.

12. This statement comes to us by way of a circuitous route from Porphyry, *Comm. in Ptolemy Harmonica* (Düring, p. 96.21–23), who quotes from Thrasyllus' work, *On the Heptachord*, who in turn cites Theophrastus as his authority.

13. Aelian is quoted by Porphyry, *Comm. in Ptolemy Harmonica* (Düring, 96.29–97.9). For examples of the left-hand technique in lyre playing, see the celebrated music lesson on the Attic skyphos by Pistoxenus in Maas and Snyder, p. 107, pl. 17. Also, Maas and Snyder, p. 74, p. 8; p. 111, pl. 28.

14. Porphyry, *Comm. in Ptolemy Harmonica* (Düring, 97.1–2).

15. On the naming of the notes, see above, Chapter 3, pp. 48–49.

16. Many scholars argue that the ancient musicians computed their scales in descending order. See, for example, Michaelides under the word *synaphe* (conjunction) for a descending analysis.

17. An *asyntheton* interval was considered "simple" because it contained no other notes within its limits. Its *asyntheton* characteristic was dictated by the laws of melodic consecution. Thus, for example, the semi-tone E–F is simple or *asyntheton* in the diatonic genus; but in the enharmonic genus it is *syntheton* or compounded

of two quarter-tone intervals: E–E+–F.

18. On this analysis, see Chailley (1956), 85–86. According to Winnington-Ingram (1928), 87–88, much of the difficulty with his analysis stems from the fact that Nicomachus assumed the scale of Philolaus to be diatonic, whereas it may have been an ancient enharmonic scale similar to a type described by Aristides Quintilianus, De mus. 1.9 (Winnington-Ingram, pp. 19–20). In any case, scholars are agreed on one point: that Philolaus' scale was a defective heptachord covering the span of an octave. Cf. Barker, II (1989), p. 261, n. 71.

19. The term diesis is defined explicitly by Nicomachus in Chapter 12 (Jan, 264.3–5) as a semi-tone, again citing Philolaus as his authority. But earlier in the same chapter (Jan, 262.22), he gives a different meaning for diesis: a half of a semi-tone, or quarter-tone, the smallest interval in the enharmonic genus. The Greek musical theorists are unanimous in applying diesis to the quarter-tone interval or, as in the case of Aristoxenus, applying the term to any interval smaller than a semi-tone. Nicomachus is our earliest authority to cite diesis as a Pythagorean term signifying semi-tone. Thereafter, it was often mentioned as such in commentaries on the Timaeus. Cf. Burkert, pp. 390–91.

20. Boethius, De inst. mus. 3.5 (Friedlein, 276.15–18).

21. The number 27 has great cosmic significance in the Timaeus and also in the Republic (587E–588A) in which 27^2 is the number of the days and nights of the year.

22. See Boethius, De inst. mus. 3.8 (Friedlein, 278.11ff.). Cf. Bower, pp. 97ff., in which Philolaus' division of the whole-tone is meticulously diagrammed.

Chapter 10

On the tuning of the notes
by means of numerical proportions

TAKING up our earlier discussion again, let me add the following to it by saying that measurements based on the lengths and thicknesses of strings and on those of the air-columns of auloi are seen to be inverse to measurements that are based on tension, in which case the smaller the term, the lower the pitch, and the greater the term, the higher the pitch. For in the former case, there is an inverse proportion in that the smaller the term, the higher is the pitch, while the greater the term, the lower is the pitch. If, therefore, one takes a long string that is kept under one and the same tension and that lies over a ruler, but is raised far enough above it so as not to touch it, and if one compares the note produced by plucking the entire string with that produced by plucking half the string—the string having been stopped by a bridge or some such contrivance at its very center so that the vibration caused by the plucking of the string may not progress beyond the half-way point—he will find the interval of an octave, the sound of half the string compared with that of the whole string being in a greater proportion, that is, in a duple proportion, a result exactly inverse to the reciprocal data of the length. And if one keeps the vibration down to a third of the string, this part having been measured off exactly, the sound from two thirds of the string will necessarily be in a hemiolic [3:2] relation to that of the sound from the whole string, or inversely proportional to the length of the string. And if one sections off a fourth part of the string, preventing the vibration from reaching any further than that, the sound from three parts of the string will be in an epitritic [4:3] relation to that of the whole string, or inversely proportional to the length of the string. So too in the case of the aulos that has three holes distributed over four equal lengths; if the holes are first stopped by the fingers and if we compared the note of the whole aulos with that produced by the middle hole, the finger being lifted from the hole, a duple proportion would be found and the note produced by the middle hole would form an octave with that of the whole aulos. The same note compared with that produced by the hole below it, namely, the hole lying next to the bottom extremity of the pipe, would stand in a hemiolic [3:2] proportion with it. This latter note, however, compared with that of the whole pipe stands in an epitritic [4:3] proportion with it. But the note produced by the hole next to the mouthpiece compared with that produced by the middle hole, stands in a duple [2:1] relation and, compared with that produced by the whole aulos, in a quadruple [4:1] relation, or inverse to the proportion of the lengths. In the case of syringes (pan-pipes), the lengths of the pipes and the widths of their bores produce a result similar to the thicknesses of the strings; for those made of two strands emit a sound in duple proportion to those made of four strands.

Commentary 10

HAVING devoted chapters five through nine to the question of the octachord—its introduction by Pythagoras, its importance to musical theory and practice, and its profound connection with mathematics—Nicomachus now returns to the subject that he had taken up earlier in Chapter 4, that of inverse proportion, the most imaginative harmonic concept in the entire mathematical arsenal of the Pythagoreans. For once armed with this concept, the Pythagoreans could deal scientifically with two factors in the production of sound that were not visible enough to the eye to be counted, and which could therefore not be measured by any tool thus far devised. Yet they were both as real as daylight. These were the factors κραδασμός, the vibratory motion of the air, and τάσις, the tension on the strings of stringed instruments and on the air in the air-columns of wind instruments.[1]

Since the Pythagoreans could not measure the actual rates of vibration, nor compute the actual amounts of tension involved in the production of pitch, they did the next best thing: they relied on their powers of inference and imagination. Basing their computations on what they could measure to a certainty—the lengths and thicknesses of strings, and the lengths and bores of air-columns—they inverted the numerical proportions that they obtained from these dimensions and arrived in this way not at the actual measurements of tension and vibration but, rather, at their correlative symptoms. In so doing, they accomplished two things: they substituted for the actual, experienced world of sound, whose causal factors could only be imagined, a geometric world made real in numbers; and, in a closely related result, they bypassed the entire problem of tension by equating it in their computations with speed of vibration.[2]

Nicomachus begins, therefore, by expounding the principle of inverse proportion and describing how it obtains between the factors size and vibration. The general context of inverse proportion having been sketched, he moves without delay to rank tension with vibration. With that done, he has no difficulty in stating that the lengths and thicknesses of strings and the lengths and bores of

air-columns—literally, the κοιλιώσεις, or "hollowed-out" sections
of auloi—stand in the same inverse relation to tension as they do
to vibration. These relations may be represented as follows:[3]

Tension:
  greater amount = greater number of vibrations = higher pitch;
  lesser amount = fewer number of vibrations = lower pitch.
Length of string or air-column:
  longer = fewer number of vibrations = lower pitch;
  shorter = greater number of vibrations = higher pitch.

With respect to these equations, the larger number on the one
standard—that of tension and vibration—represents the higher
pitch, while the larger number on the other standard—that of
dimension—represents the lower pitch.

By contrasting stringed instruments with winds, as he does so
carefully in this chapter, Nicomachus was able to demonstrate that
the principle of inverse proportion is not only consistent mathematically, but that it comports with the known facts of musical
pitch. As he emphasizes, then, there is, on the one hand, a mathematical consistency between the numerical ratios and their reciprocal relations, while on the other, there is a musical consistency
between the dimensions of the sounding instrument and the pitch
it produces. That being the case, Nicomachus cannot remind his
reader often enough that inverse proportion obtains whenever
musical instruments speak, whether they be winds or strings. And
he drives home this point using a great variety of terms, terms
which carry the sense of "inverse" or "converse" or "reverse,"
"opposite" or "contrary," as the case may be: ἐναντίον, ἀντίστροφον,
ἀνάπαλιν, ἐναντιοπαθῶς, ἀνταποδόσεσιν, ἀντιστρόφως, ἐναντίως, ἀντιπαθῶς.

Nicomachus begins his demonstration of inverse proportion in
action by describing an experiment with the monochord, the
acoustical instrument par excellence appropriate for this purpose.
In accord with his directions, in which he virtually tells his reader
how to construct a working monochord, we can imagine a string
stretched between two stationary bridges and raised above a graduated ruler or "canon," the vibrating portion of the string being

controlled by a movable bridge. This may be diagrammed as follows:[4]

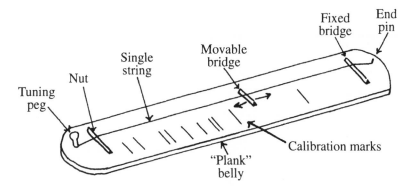

Figure 3. A Simple Monochord

As can be seen, two calibrations are involved, in one of which a larger number on one scale (that of vibration) is associated with a higher pitch, while in the other a larger number on the other scale (that of length) is associated with a lower pitch. Conversely, a smaller number on the one scale (that of vibration) is associated with a lower pitch, while a smaller number on the other scale (that of length) is associated with a higher pitch. Pursuing Nicomachus' explanation, the vibrating portion of a string stopped at its mid-point will move twice as fast as the string vibrating in its full length. Thus, in the case of an octave, the vibration is in the ratio of 2:1, while the length of the string shows a reciprocal relation in the fraction 1/2. According to this calculation, the larger number represents the greater speed of vibration. In the case of a fifth, i.e. the interval produced by stopping a third of the string, the vibrating portion of the string will be 2/3 of the entire string, but the vibration producing the higher pitch will be, relative to that of the lower pitch, in a ratio of 3:2, or the reciprocal of the length of the string. In the case of a fourth, the interval produced by stopping one quarter of the string, the vibrating portion of the string will be 3/4 of the entire string, but the vibration producing the higher pitch will be, relative to that of the lower, in a ratio of 4:3, or the reciprocal of the length of the string. Thus, if the terms 6:8:9:12, adopted by Nicomachus in Chapter 6, are construed according to the facts presented by him here, they must represent the factor vibration.

Nicomachus' main point in setting up this experiment with a stretched string is to emphasize the mathematical reciprocity between string length and string vibration. And his numerical assignments reflect this intention. For the sequence 6:8:9:12 represents the inferred rate of vibration productive of the notes hypate (E), mese (A), paramese (B), and nete (E¹). In other words, these terms are the reciprocals of the lengths of string that are allowed to vibrate. Other accounts that deal with similar experiments with strings keep the focus not on vibration, as does Nicomachus, but instead on the string lengths themselves, with the consequence that the results adduced are the inverse of those obtained by Nicomachus. The most scientifically detailed of these other accounts is that of Ptolemy who, in his *Harmonica*, explains a procedure involving an initial bisecting of a string which has been stretched over two stationary bridges. One half of the string is used as the constant, while the other half is divided into the proper harmonic segments by a movable bridge. This arrangement, an example of the canonic method, is based on the assumption that any two commensurable magnitudes on a straight line can find their equivalence in a corresponding interval between two musical notes. In this case, the frame of reference is the *diastema*—that "distance," or continuous extension on the canon, whose relation to another "distance," or commensurably continuous extension on the canon, is expressible as a *logos*, or numerical ratio.[5]

This process, as the Pythagoreans showed, if applied to two commensurable distances or magnitudes, produces the largest common measure. However, when the magnitudes are measured on the canon, if the lesser of two unequal magnitudes is successively subtracted from the greater, the consequence will be that that magnitude which is left over will never measure the one before it; in other words, the magnitudes will be incommensurable.[6] So that since, where musical intervals are concerned, the process of subtraction never comes to an end, there can be no common measure. Thus, as Philolaus demonstrated in his division of the whole-tone, there is at the very start of the process already a remainder (*leimma*), and this surplus of measure persists until it becomes so minute that the process must be brought to a halt.

Nicomachus next examines the principle of inverse proportion as it applies to wind instruments and demonstrates that it applies in much the same way as in stringed instruments. Thus he shows that air-columns, such as those of auloi or syringes, behave like stretched strings in that the greater their dimensions the lower their pitch, and conversely. He goes on to explain that the finger-hole by which the octave is produced was bored in the middle of the air-column and thus that the ratio of the octave (2:1) represents the proportion of the entire air-column to that of its half. The hole which produces the fifth is so placed that the length of the entire pipe and that portion above the hole are in a ratio of 3:2. The hole which produces a fourth is so placed that the entire pipe and the portion above the hole are in a ratio of 4:3. What is clear thus far in Nicomachus' account is that the finger-holes perform the same function in pipes as do the fingers that stop the stretched string; that is, like a stretched string freely vibrating in its total length, an air-column with all its holes closed produces a fundamental pitch. And this pitch depends principally on the length of the air-column. The length of the air column is altered by opening or closing the finger-holes, the rise in pitch being proportional to the shortening of the column.

Taking up Nicomachus' aulos example, if we assume that the diameter of the finger-holes is equal to the internal diameter of the pipe, the positions of the holes as described by Nicomachus are what we would expect in an instrument of cylindrical bore. To be sure, Nicomachus says nothing about the fact that the extent to which the pipe of the aulos is shortened depends on the relation of the area of the hole to the cross-sectional area of the pipe's bore, and also on the thickness of the wall through which the hole is bored. In any case, however, let us suppose that the sound produced by Nicomachus' aulos with all its holes closed is F.[7] If each hole is opened in the direction of the mouthpiece, these holes, positioned as Nicomachus describes it, should yield the following:[8]

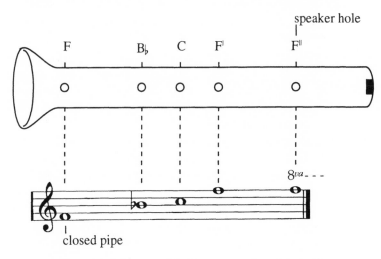

Figure 4. A Pipe Divided into Four Equal Lengths

Thus, the B♭ hole is placed at one quarter the distance from the lower end of the pipe, the C hole at one third the distance, and the F hole at one half the distance. To these holes Nicomachus adds another next to the mouthpiece, which produces a note two octaves higher than that of the entire pipe and one octave higher than the note of the middle hole. Moreover, this added hole, near the mouthpiece, like the "speaker" hole of the clarinet, would when open raise the tone of each hole to the first harmonic, or an octave.[9] In this case it produces the first harmonic of the note produced by the middle hole. Nicomachus' purpose in this demonstration is to show that the speed of movement of the air in the column of this instrument is in inverse proportion to the length of the air-column. To this extent, then, inverse proportion, according to Nicomachus, works in much the same way with winds as it does with strings. In taking this position he is in full agreement with Ps.-Aristotle, *Prob.* 19.23, in which the following statement appears:

Why is nete the duple of hypate? Is it first of all because a string when plucked at half of its length produces an octave with the string that is plucked at its full length? The case is similar with syringes: for the sound produced by the middle hole of the syrinx forms an octave with that produced by the whole syrinx. In the case of auloi also the octave is obtained by a duple interval, and those who bore the holes in auloi obtain the octave in this way. Similarly, the fifth is obtained with the hemiolic [3:2] ratio ... and the fourth with the epitritic [4:3] ratio.[10]

Nicomachus concludes the chapter by suggesting that the size of the bores in air-columns is a factor equivalent in function to thickness in strings. In each case, the greater the dimension, the lower the pitch. Thus, the vibration of a two-stranded string, that is, a string made of two parts (δίκωλοι) is in a ratio of 2:1 to that of a four-stranded string, or a string made of four parts (τετρακώλων), and the former produces the higher octave.[11] In other words, changing the thickness of strings produces the same effect as increasing their length. This principle is, of course, a fundamental one in the art of piano construction. For if the piano-builder relied merely on the laws of string length to compass all the pitches in the musical range, the longest string of his piano would have to be more than 150 times the length of the shortest. To avoid such contingencies he avails himself of the principle of inverse proportion. By wrapping the bass strings of the piano with thin copper wire, he obtains the desired frequencies without having to increase the length of the strings.[12]

Notes to Chapter 10

1. Tension on strings produces vibrations which are approximately at right angles to the length of the string and are called, accordingly, transverse vibrations. Tension exerted on the air in wind instruments produces air motions that are parallel to the pipe length and are called longitudinal vibrations. On the vibrations of strings, see Jeans, pp. 81ff.; on the vibrations of air-columns, see Jeans, pp. 109ff.

2. See Levin (1990), 437–38. Cf. Chapter 4 above, pp. 66–67.

3. Jeans, pp. 112–13: "Thus the free vibrations of a column of air are exactly analogous to those of a stretched string . . . the period of each vibration is exactly proportional to the length of the column of air which is vibrating." The fundamental pitch of an air-column, like that of a stretched string, depends principally on its length and the thickness of the column itself. Since the vibrations producing the fundamental pitch have frequencies that stand in the ratios 1:2:3:4, "natural concordant harmonics" are also produced together with the fundamental, these contributing to the tonal quality of the pitch. See Jeans, pp. 123–24.

4. Cf. Jeans, pp. 62–64. On the mathematical principles underlying experiments with the stretched string, see Fideler in Guthrie (1988), pp. 24–28.

5. See Barker, II (1989), pp. 292–93; cf. Levin (1990), 441–42.

6. This geometrical criterion for the incommensurability of two magnitudes on the canon is provided by Euclid, *Elements*.10.2 (Heath, 3, p. 17): "If, when the less of two unequal magnitudes is continually subtracted in turn from the greater, that which is left never measures the one before it, the magnitudes will be incommensurable."

7. Sound production in wind instruments is far more complex than Nicomachus' description suggests. Thus, for example, the modes of free vibration in air-columns differ according as the pipe is "open" or "stopped"; the frequency of vibration is also dependent on numerous factors such as the material of the pipe, its shape, the relation of the diameter of the pipe to its length, etc. On these factors, see Benade, pp. 209ff. The mouth-piece or lack of one plays a considerable role also in the production of pitch. For example, two open pipes of identical length but of different bores do not give the same pitch if played

without a reed. But a stopped cylindrical pipe such as the aulos would sound an octave below the pitch of a similar pipe that is open at both ends. For these and other relations, see Schlesinger, pp. 82–87.

8. The assumption here is that Nicomachus' aulos is a closed-pipe whose fundamental pitch is produced with all the finger-holes closed. For a pipe with these properties, see Schlesinger, p. 87. Unfortunately, no treatise on the boring of pipes has been preserved. Indeed, several are mentioned by Athenaeus 4.182C, which must have dealt extensively with the subject. The loss of the definitive treatise by Aristoxenus, *On the Boring of Auloi*, in several volumes, is, of course the most regrettable of all. See Athenaeus 14.634C.

9. The "speaker" hole is discussed by Howard, pp. 31–35. On the function of "speaker" holes, see also Benade, pp. 225–27. Cf. Barker, II (1989), p. 108, n. 42.

10. Similarly, Theon (Hiller, 60.18ff). Cf. R. and D. Lawlor, p. 40; Barker, II (1989), p. 119.

11. Barker, II, p. 263, n. 76 refers these words to pipe widths and suggests that "the pipes of the *syrinx* were sometimes made up of different numbers of pieces, each of the same size, *but the inference is insecure*" (italics mine). Since Nicomachus is contrasting the thickness of pipes with that of strings, it seems reasonable to refer these words to strings made of more than one strand. It is in this sense that Ps-Aristotle, *De audibilibus* 804b, speaks of "badly plaited strings." See Barker, II (1989), p. 108. In any case, weight of strings is a factor equivalent to volume of air in pipes in the production of pitch alteration. For discussion, see Schlesinger, pp. 83–84.

12. See Jeans, p. 65.

Chapter 11

On the double octave in the diatonic genus

THIS, then, is the diagrammatic structure of the scale in the diatonic genus, consisting of a double octave of quadruple breadth. For this is all that the voice at full capacity encompasses without any insecurity or vacillation, it being difficult for the voice to place itself at either extreme. On the one hand, the voice has a tendency to hoot like a cuckoo in the treble register, while on the other hand, it tends to buzz in the deeper register of the bass notes.

Accordingly, to the old-fashioned lyre, that is, to the heptachord composed of two tetrachords in conjunction—the mese itself delimiting both of the consonant intervals, the lower one contingent on hypate as one ascends, the higher one contingent on nete as one descends—to these they attached two other tetrachords, one at each extremity. Adjoining the original nete the hyperbolaion tetrachord was situated, called "hyperbolaion" because it was composed of a higher and "transcending" vocal register, beginning from the ancient nete, again by conjunction with it. Consequently, the extended tetrachord found its limit after three notes only had been added which were suitably named as follows: trite hyperbolaion, then paranete hyperbolaion, then nete of the same tetrachord.

In order that the tetrachord preceding it [hyperbolaion] and formed by conjunction with the mese, might have its notes so designated as to distinguish it from the hyperbolaion, its notes were given these names: after mese comes trite synemmenon, then paranete synemmenon, then nete synemmenon. And the entire high-pitched range reckoning from the mese itself necessarily completes a heptachord also. To the original hypate they added at the bass the other of the tetrachords mentioned, again by conjunction, the ancient hypate being also comprehended in it since it is the higher of the notes in the tetrachord. In a similar way, for the sake of distlnguishing it from the disposition of the prior tetrachord, this one also acquired more distinctive names. For to each name was added the word, "hypaton," such as: hypate hypaton, parhypate hypaton, diatonos hypaton or lichanos hypaton, for it makes no difference which of the two names we use.

And this entire system from the mese to the hypate of the hypaton tetrachord turns out to be a heptachord composed of two conjunct tetrachords, these using one common note, the ancient hypate. Consequently, from hypate hypaton to nete hyperbolaion there are four conjunct tetrachords. A thirteen-stringed system is found, the seventh string being fixed diatonically from either end. Then, as we said previously, those intending to vary the attunement intercalated the eighth note at a distance of a whole-tone between mese and the ancient trite (or, as some say, between trite and paranete) and clearly emphasized the interval of a fifth. And the mese was found to be no longer truly a middle note. For in the case of strings that are fixed to an equal number of degrees, there cannot be one middle note, but necessarily two, the seventh and eighth strings.

Again, they added one outermost note below the hypate, the lowest of the existing notes, which they called because of this "addition," proslambanomenos, it too being at a distance of a whole-tone below the hypate hypaton as one descends basswards. The purpose of this addition was that the systems on either side of the mese might be octachords, and that the mese might truly be a middle note by being situated among fifteen notes as the eighth string from either end; and that the double octave, the total compass of the scale, might be a doubly duple proportion, that is, a quadruple proportion; and that the order of names, moving upward in succession, might be such as follow:

proslambanomenos
then after an interval of a whole-tone, hypate hypaton
then after a semi-tone, parhypate hypaton
then after a whole-tone, lichanos hypaton, named after
    the finger of the left hand, the finger next to the thumb,
    which is called forefinger and is
    always applied to this string
then after another whole-tone, hypate meson

following in succession after a semi-tone, parhypate meson
and after a whole-tone, lichanos meson, which they
    also call "diatonos," naming it after the
    diatonic genus itself
then after another whole-tone, mese
then paramesos, after a whole-tone
then trite diezeugmenon, after a semi-tone
then after a whole-tone, paranete diezeugmenon
and after another whole-tone, nete diezeugmenon
succeeding this, after a semi-tone, trite hyperbolaion
then after a whole-tone, paranete hyperbolaion
and following upon all, after a whole-tone, nete hyperbolaion

In reminiscence of the original conjunction in the heptachord,
another tetrachord called synemmenon was inserted between the
meson tetrachord and the diezeugmenon, complete with its own
trite, separated by a semi-tone from the mese; then after a whole-
tone, its own paranete, then after another whole-tone, the conjunctive nete of exactly the same pitch and the same sound as the
disjunctive paranete. Consequently, there are five tetrachords in
all, hypaton, meson, synemmenon, diezeugmenon, hyperbolaion—
among which there are two disjunctions and three conjunctions.
The disjunctions occur between the synemmenon and the
hyperbolaion tetrachords and between the meson and the
diezeugmenon tetrachords, each comprising the interval of a whole-
tone—and the three conjunctions, one conjoining hypaton with
meson, one conjoining meson itself to synemmenon, and the last
one conjoining diezeugmenon to hyperbolaion.

    The discoveries of all these elements note by note, their causes
and developments, how they came about, by whom they were
discovered and when, and from what type of origin, I shall explain
to you in my extensive treatment, beginning with the tetrachord
and ending with the complete *katapyknosis* of the octave, not only
in this diatonic genus, but also in the chromatic and the enharmonic,
together with the testimonies of ancient witnesses who are the
most reliable and who are held in the highest esteem. And in

addition we shall set forth the division of the so-called Pythagorean canon up to the twenty-seventh multiple, in rigorous conformity with the intention of this master, not as Eratosthenes or Thrasyllus misrepresented it, but as the Locrian Timaeus rendered it, whom even Plato followed closely.

Commentary 11

THROUGHOUT the whole of antiquity, the mathematical harmonics of the Pythagoreans and the individual practices of musicians—much like the conflicting tenets of science and religion—existed in a state of uneasy tension. Among the Pythagoreans, as Nicomachus has explained thus far in the *Manual*, harmonic cohesion was secured by adherence to the principles of mathematics; even musicians like Philolaus, Archytas and, centuries later, Ptolemy, could see no merit in any other kind of allegiance. The degree to which the freedom of the individual musician was compromised by his duty to the laws of Pythagorean harmonics must have varied considerably, however. For some, the mathematical imperatives of Pythagorean harmonic science had to be preserved at all costs. To this end they sought a minimum unit measure with which they could fix the size of all the intervals in their melodic vocabularies. This was a vain pursuit, however, given over to countless hours of "tormenting," as Plato put it, "the strings of their lyres and trying to wring the truth out of them by twisting them on their tuning-pegs."[1] Other musicians, meanwhile, were trying to find ways to adapt the diverse musical practices of peoples from all parts of the world—Lydians, Phrygians, Ionians, Aeolians—to their own particular needs and desires. For them, the problem was how to play the many different melodic modes on a single instrument without having to retune for each mode. And as they apparently saw it, the problems raised by the Pythagorean principles—for example, that connected with the semi-tone—were mere subtleties that could be dealt with by the use of imaginative tunings and scale-structures.

Solutions by practicing musicians to such problems were in fact being worked out long before the technical writers on music supplied the theory that validated those efforts. In this development, two distinct stages need to be recognized: the one before the technical innovations of Aristoxenus, and that after he codified the elements and principles of the musicians' practice into a coherent and systematic theory of music. It is this commonality in Aristoxenus' theory that accounts for its long survival and the reformulation it underwent in the writings of such theorists as Cleonides, Gaudentius, Bacchius, Aristides Quintilianus, Nicomachus and—centuries later in the Byzantine era—Pachymeres and Manuel Bryennius. As I observed earlier in the commentary to Chapter 2 of the *Manual*, Aristoxenus' theory did not occur in a vacuum: it grew out of Aristotelian thought, and it responded to the musical heritage of the Greeks. Now, in the final two chapters of his *Manual*, Nicomachus returns to the subject and details the various steps that culminated in the Aristoxenian theory of rnusic.

As Nicomachus explains in this chapter, there were numerous stages that led to the final standardization of the two-octave scale, and they were all dictated by one factor: the capacity of the human voice. This capacity, he maintains, comprises two octaves, and any pitches that exceeded this range introduced distortions of the worst possible kind: hoots and screeches in the treble, and buzzing rasps in the bass; in other words, sounds ineligible for any musical purposes. Aristoxenus, it should be noted, was somewhat less conservative in assessing the voice's capabilities; he considered two octaves and a fifth to be an optimal range.[2] In any case, Nicomachus' point is that, at the extremes of its range, the voice is incapable of producing the individual and discretely-articulated pitches necessary for the creation of music. When he makes this point in *Excerpt* 4, he uses even more extreme imagery: there he likens the overreaching voice in the bass to the bellowing of cows, and the overstraining voice in the treble to the hooting of cuckoos and, even worse, to the howling of wolves. Interestingly enough, Nicomachus' younger contemporary, Ptolemy, has something very similar to say about the sounds of the voice at the extremes of the pitch range:

> Such sounds as they co-occur with the very movements that strain upward or, again, with those that resolve downward are, as they end up in the bass, like the bellowing of cows, and in the treble like the howling of wolves.[3]

The question as to who was quoting whom, will probably never be answered with any degree of certainty. The likelihood that it was

Nicomachus who was quoting Ptolemy in this connection is, to be sure, somewhat increased by the appearance of Ptolemy's name in *Excerpt 4*. But whatever the case, one thing seems certain: both Nicomachus and Ptolemy were in agreement where the standardized two octave Immutable System (Σύστημα τέλειον ἀμετάβολον) is concerned. For as they saw it, this system not only provided the most comfortable range for the human voice but, in its final standardized form, it also contained all the elements necessary for the production of the seven-octave species of Aristoxenus.[4]

According to Nicomachus, the standardized two-octave scale resulted from a series of gradual extensions of the ancient heptachord—that scale described in Chapters 3 and 5 as comprising two tetrachords conjoined on the note mese. In other words, this was the scale that existed prior to Pythagoras' creation of the octachord. To the two tetrachords of this conjunct scale—the one called meson, or the notes of the "middle" tetrachord, the other synemmenon or notes of the "conjunct" tetrachord, two additions were made: that is, a complete tetrachord was added to each end of the heptachord. This resulted, as Nicomachus says, in a scale consistlng of four conjunct tetrachords and thirteen notes:

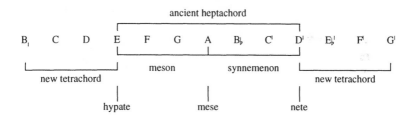

Since each of these tetrachords is identical in form—semi-tone, whole-tone, whole-tone—it was necessary, as Nicomachus explains, to distinguish the one from the other by identifying its particular position in the scale. Thus, the higher tetrachord, formed by conjunction on the ancient nete synemmenon (D), was called hyperbolaion, or tetrachord "of the highest notes," while the lower one, added at the bass to the ancient hypate meson (E), was called

hypaton, or tetrachord "of the lowest notes."[5] With each of these
tetrachords now identified according to its position in the scale, it
becomes possible to single out any note of the scale within each of
the tetrachords. Accordingly, hypate hypaton is B_l, parhypate
hypaton is C, lichanos hypaton (or diatonos as it is sometimes
called in the diatonic genus) is D.

As Nicomachus has it then, these tetrachordal extensions to the
ancient heptachord resulted in a thirteen-note scale in which mese
(A) was the seventh note from each extremity and each tetrachord
was connected to the other by conjunction. His analysis of this
scale is so clear and carefully outlined that he leaves no question in
the mind of the reader as to its structure. At the same time,
however, his analysis raises serious problems, one of the more
obvious being that it ill accords with the information presented in
Chapter 5. In that chapter Nicomachus made a point of emphasiz-
ing that Pythagoras was responsible for the very first alteration of
the heptachord, which alteration extended its range to a full octave.
Here, however, he takes no account at all of the Pythagorean
octachord. Equally serious is the fact that in the work of no other
theorist is mention made of a thirteen note scale such as that
detailed by Nicomachus. True, the Byzantine theorist Pachymeres
speaks of such a system, but inasmuch as his information was
obtained from none other than Nicomachus, his testimony cannot
be taken seriously.[6] Finally, Nicomachus' description of this devel-
oping thirteen-note scale cannot even be reconciled with the facts
presented by him in Excerpt 4. As he states the case here in Chapter
11, the thirteen-note scale resulted from the addition of two whole
tetrachords to the ancient heptachord. But in Excerpt 4 he says that
the extensions were made not to the heptachord, but to the
octachord, and that they were in the form not of entire tetrachords
but, rather, of individual notes, the addition of each such note, or
string to the lyre, being the work of an individual musician,
Prophrastus having added a ninth string, Histiaeus a tenth, and
Timotheos an eleventh.

These extensions, according to Nicomachus in Excerpt 4, eventually produced a scale of eighteen notes, prompting the comic poet
Pherecrates, to indict in scathing terms these innovations and the
musicians responsible for them. In one of those fortunate coinci-

dences, the very passage to which Nicomachus referred has come
down to us. In it Pherecrates has just placed Music—personified as
a woman—on stage. She makes her entrance in complete disarray,
her body bearing marks of recent outrage. Justice asks her what has
happened to her, and she replies with these words:

> I will tell you willingly. It will be a pleasure for me to tell you and
> for you to hear. My troubles began with Melanippides who was
> the first of them; grabbing me, he pushed me down and made me
> go slack with twelve strings. Nonetheless, he was passable com-
> pared with the ills I now have. That cursed Cinesias of Attica has
> so destroyed me with his eccentrically out-of-tune twists in his
> strophes that in the dithyrambs that he composes the left side
> looks like the right, as in a reflecting shield. Yet, I could still stand
> him. But Phrynis put in his own kind of screwball, bending and
> twisting me until I was totally undone, with twelve tunings on his
> pentachords. But even he was tolerable to me. For if he blundered,
> he repaired his errors later. But, my dear, Timotheos has buried
> me and crushed me to pieces most shamefully. . . . What man is
> this Timotheos? He is a red-headed Milesian who has caused me
> evils beyond those of all the others I have mentioned, introducing
> his perverse ant-tracks; and when he came upon me while I was
> walking alone, he undid me and unfastened me with his twelve
> strings.[7]

Writing at his distance from these musical events of the fifth
century B.C.E., Nicomachus could regard with a theoretician's
neutrality what struck Pherecrates as utterly abominable. Indeed,
Pherecrates speaks much like someone in the Paris audience of the
early twentieth century upon hearing the first performance of
Stravinsky's *Rite of Spring*. The vehemence of that audience's
reaction to Stravinsky's musical innovations would have been very
understandable to Pherecrates and, what is more, to Plato as well.
For a hundred years or so after composers like Timotheos were
offending Pherecrates, Plato was still inveighing against these
"moderns," with their many strings and their multiple modula-
tions.[8]

But musicians, as Nicomachus seems to have intuited, were

never constrained by the conservative tastes of poets and philosophers, or by the orthodoxy of musical theorists. If they felt the need
to modulate from one mode to another, they would extend the
range of their instruments to accomodate a new mode; and they
would do so without compunction, as did Ion of Chios, for example,
who early in the fifth century B.C.E. added an eleventh string to his
lyre.[9] And when Timotheos, the enfant terrible of Greek music, did
the same thing independently of Ion, the Spartans were said to have
condemned him for his audacity and actually to have hung up his
offending instrument in the Scias, the meeting-place of the Spartan
Assembly. It was still hanging there in the second century C.E.,
where Pausanius claimed to have seen it.[10]

What is especially interesting about Timotheos' eleven-stringed
lyre is the way in which he brought it into being. For unlike Ion,
who apparently had only to add a single string to produce a
hendecachord, Timotheos was said to have added four strings at
one time to the ancient heptachord.[11] In other words, what he did
tends to confirm the evidence of Nicomachus, i.e. that he added an
entire tetrachord to the ancient and hallowed heptachord. It is even
conceivable that Timotheos added this tetrachord by disjunction
with the ancient nete (D), a tetrachord improperly called hyperbolaion by Nicomachus, producing a scale of the following sort:

E   F   G   A   B♭   C'   D'   E'   F'   G'   A'

Thus when Nicomachus speaks of musicians adding whole
tetrachords at a time to the ancient heptachord, his words, however
much they may conflict with his own testimony in *Excerpt* 4, in
fact find important confirmation in the story of Timotheos'
hendecachord.

Referring to his earlier discussion in Chapter 5 concerning
Pythagoras' invention of the octachord, Nicomachus now takes up
the question of how Pythagoras' octachordal scale, with its emphasis on the pentachord, was incorporated into the two-octave scale.[12]
To begin with, he says that the insertion of the whole-tone between

A (mese) and the ancient trite (C), as some theorists analyze it or, as others see it, between the ancient trite (B♭) and paranete (C), caused a major change in the position of mese; that is, once this whole-tone insertion was effected, mese could no longer occupy a middle position in the scale but had, instead, to share this function with paramese. In other words, the seventh note from either end of the scale is no longer A, but is, rather, A and B, respectively:

$$B_{\scriptstyle|}\ \ C\ \ D\ \ E\ \ F\ \ G\ \ A\ \ B\ \ C^{\scriptstyle|}\ D^{\scriptstyle|}\ E^{\scriptstyle|}\ F^{\scriptstyle|}\ G^{\scriptstyle|}\ A^{\scriptstyle|}$$

$$\longleftarrow \underline{} \ \underline{} \longrightarrow$$
$$\qquad\quad 7 \qquad\ 7$$

But by adding at the bass a note an octave lower than mese, a note literally "taken in addition" (proslambanomenos), there resulted a complete octachord on either side of mese. This scale was called the Greater Perfect System (Σύστημα τέλειον μεῖζον).[13]

One of the problems with Nicomachus' explanation thus far is his failure to deal with the presence in his thirteen-note scale of the tetrachord hyperbolaion (D E♭ F G). Instead, he leaves it to the reader to infer that this tetrachord had to be shifted upward by a whole-tone (i.e. to E F G A') in order to make room for the Pythagorean disjunction between A–B, and this regardless of whether it was said to come between B♭ and C or between A and C. For as it turns out, the tetrachord originally spanning D–G in the thirteen-note scale must now occupy the distance between E–A'. This result, however, must be gleaned from the listing by Nicomachus of the entire scale, note by note and tetrachord by tetrachord.

Once the Greater Perfect System was organized, the original conjunctive tetrachord (synemmenon) that had figured so prominently in the ancient heptachord was not to be discarded. On the contrary, according to Nicomachus, it was preserved intact well within the framework of the Greater Perfect System, the resultant set of relations now providing a paradigmatic tuning system adequate to serve all musical purposes. This paradigmatic scale was called the Immutable, or Changeless System.[14] And as we can see from Nicomachus' analysis, it comprises five tetrachords, two whole-tone disjunctions an octave apart, and three semi-tone conjunctions. The entire system appears as follows:

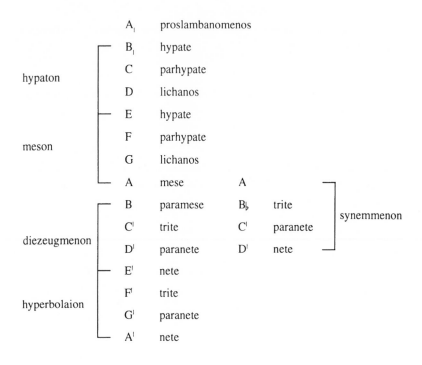

Figure 5. The Greater Perfect System

Thus far, Nicomachus' analysis of these theoretical developments has concerned one melodic genus only: the diatonic, that genus in which the progressions are literally "through the whole-tones." His promise to explain the other genera—the chromatic and the enharmonic—is partially fulfilled in Chapter 12, where he locates the notes in the three genera, tetrachord by tetrachord. In this way he provides a complete *katapyknosis*—a diagram in which all the intervals, including the smallest quarter-tones, appear "packed together" in each octave.[15] He then promises his reader a historical survey of these theoretical developments over the centuries, and an explanation of how they culminated in the two-octave set of relations which he has here depicted—relations which he says can be represented mathematically on the canon.

To understand these relations within the two-octave Immutable System, it is necessary, according to Nicomachus, to understand their mathematical background. And this, he says, can best be done by consulting the division of the canon—κατατομὴ κανόνος, or canonis sectio—that was established according to Pythagorean doctrine. In providing his reader with a model of the sectio canonis in two octaves and in all three genera, he states that he will not consult Eratosthenes or Thrasyllus, since they have both misrepresented the traditional Pythagorean method. Considering the reputations of these two figures, Nicomachus' charges against them are somewhat surprising. Thrasyllus, for example, the author of a work on the Heptachord, was a man deeply versed in Pythagorean and Platonic philosophy; he was also the personal astrologer to the Emperor Tiberius from about 6 B.C.E. on.[16] And Eratosthenes (c. 275–194 B.C.E.), the chief librarian of the celebrated library at Alexandria, was an astronomer and scientist of prodigious accomplishments: his estimation of the earth's diameter at 7850 miles, for example, was only about 50 miles short of the truth.[17] Since these were not the sort of scholars to be dismissed lightly, Nicomachus must have felt that he had good reasons to find fault with their divisions of the canon. We can only speculate at what those reasons might have been.

In the case of Thrasyllus, we know enough of his canonical method from the testimony of Theon to surmise why Nicomachus found it objectionable: it is in all respects decidedly non-Pythagorean. Thus, Thrasyllus did not begin, as did the Pythagoreans, with the harmonic ratios of the concordant intervals; instead, he used the number 12 as his sole point of reference, and by dividing the canon into 12 equal segments he was able to locate the following notes of the scale:[18]

12	A$_\iota$	proslambanomenos
11	B	hypate hypaton
10		
9	D	lichanos hypaton
8	E	hypate meson
7		
6	A	mese
5		
4	E$^\iota$	nete diezeugmenon
3	A$^\iota$	nete hyperbolaion
2		
1		

Figure 6. Thrasyllus' Division of the Canon

On Thrasyllus' linear construction, the ratio of nete diezeugmenon (E$^\iota$) to nete hyperbolaion (A$^\iota$) is thus 4:3, or that of a fourth. The ratio of mese (A) to nete hyperbolaion (A$^\iota$) is 6:3, or 2:1, the ratio of the octave; the ratio of hypate meson (E) to nete hyperbolaion (A$^\iota$) is 8:3, the octave and a fourth. Lichanos (D) relative to the same nete hyperbolaion (A$^\iota$) is represented by 9:3, or 3:1, the ratio of an octave and a fifth. And the ratio 12:3 = 4:1 represents the distance from proslambanomenos (A$_\iota$) to nete hyperbolaion (A$^\iota$), or the double octave in duple proportion. The internal terms are 6:4 = 3:2 (A–E$^\iota$), the fifth; 8:6 = 4:3 (E–A), the fourth; 9:6 = 3:2 (D–A), the fifth; 12:6 = 2:1 proslambanomenos A$_\iota$ to mese A), the octave; 9:8 (D–E), the whole-tone.

Nicomachus' criticism of Eratosthenes' procedure is harder to rationalize, especially since Eratosthenes' work called *Platonicus* was not only a commentary on Plato's *Timaeus*, but was also a probable source for Nicomachus himself in his *Introduction to Arithmetic*.[19] What is more, the computations by which Eratosthenes determined the form of the diatonic tetrachord are identical to those of Plato in the *Timaeus*, i.e. 256:243, 9:8, 9:8. There are two possible explanations, it seems: Nicomachus faulted Eratosthenes for limiting his computations to the tetrachord; or, more likely, he found Eratosthenes' computations of the highest enharmonic interval at 19:15 to be distinctly un-Pythagorean.[20]

According to Nicomachus, there was only one proper way to segment the canon: that was to bring it up to four octaves and a major sixth, i.e. to the twenty-seventh multiple, or 27:1, just as Plato had done in the *Timaeus*. As Nicomachus has it here, Plato did not himself invent this procedure but learned it from Timaeus of Locrus, the purported individual after whom Plato's dialogue was named. That Timaeus was a character made up by Plato to play the role of a philosopher and scientist of the western school—a supposition held by many—had quite obviously never occurred to Nicomachus. For Nicomachus there was no question as to the identity of Timaeus; he was just as Socrates described him in the *Timaeus*:[21] a well-born citizen, affluent, the holder of the highest offices in the city, sharer in the highest honors, and a philosopher of towering stature. By way of confirming the historical existence of Timaeus, Nicomachus relied on other evidence as well: first, centuries of gossip that made of Plato's *Timaeus* a plagiarization of a work written originally by a historical personage of that name and, second, a treatise entitled *On the Soul of the World* that came down to Nicomachus under the name Timaeus Locrus.[22]

The stories retailing Plato's reputed plagiarism of the *Timaeus* seem to have been rampant in antiquity and go back as far as the fourth century B.C.E. One such story, told by the satirist Timon of Phlius (c. 325–c. 235 B.C.E.) has Plato actually expending a substantial sum of money to purchase a little book called *Timaeus*.[23] Another, told by Diogenes Laertius, has Plato buying the *Timaeus* from relatives of Philolaus for 40 pieces of silver.[24] Although it cannot be known for certain why such stories were circulated about Plato and the *Timaeus*, one can suggest as a possible motive the desire to discredit Plato as the inventor of the *Timaeus* scale, a scale carried to the twenty-seventh multiple, and one which the Pythagoreans themselves ought to have devised. For it is in the *Timaeus* scale that the precepts of Pythagoras are given their most complete and fully realized expression.

The claim by Nicomachus in Chapter 11 of a dubious background for Plato's twenty-seventh multiple loses some of its force by what he says in *Excerpt 5*. For there he speaks of this very canonic segmentation as being entirely compatible not only with the philosophy of Pythagoras but, what is more, as being consistent also with Plato's general harmonic theory. Leaving aside this apparent discrepancy, we may point to additional difficulties that are introduced in *Excerpt 7*. Here Nicomachus injects a completely new idea with a reference to a *Psychogonia*, in which the integer adopted is not 27, as in Plato's *Timaeus*, but 36, the number that appears in the spurious treatise *Timaeus Locrus*. Nicomachus goes on to suggest that the sectioning of the canon detailed in this treatise provided a genuinely Pythagorean model for Plato. But if this *Psychogonia* was indeed the source from which Plato derived his segmentation of the canon in the *Timaeus*, why did Plato adopt 27 as his multiple and not 36? Indeed, as Nicomachus could not have failed to notice, the two works—Plato's *Timaeus* and the treatise known as *Timaeus Locrus*—are in fundamental disaccord on the question of the canonic segmentation; there is no way to arrive at a harmonic construction of four octaves and a major sixth as Plato did in the *Timaeus* and still get the thirty-six terms of the *Timaeus Locrus*.[25] Yet, from what he says about his promised longer work, it was just such a construction that Nicomachus meant to attempt: that is, a reconciliation between the *Timaeus* scale of Plato and that of the *Timaeus Locrus*. Encouraging him in such a quixotic task would have been his belief in the harmonic properties of the number 36. It is, for one thing, the square of the first perfect number—6; even more important, it is the sum of the terms in the harmonic ratios: 6:8:9:12, and their common source, the monad.[26] Quite possibly, it is the reconciliation between this 36 and Plato's 27 that Nicomachus was planning to bring about, and we may be glimpsing him here in the earliest stages of this enterprise.

Notes to Chapter 11

1. Plato, *Rep.*, 531B1–4. Cf. Chapter 6 above, p. 96, n. 11.

2. Aristoxenus, *Harm. El.* 1.20 (Da Rios, 26.29–30).

3. It is probable that Ptolemy wrote his *Almagest*, one of the greatest works of Greek astronomy, sometime during the reign of Antoninus Pius (138–61 C.E.), an assumption made probable by Ptolemy himself. For certain of the observations recorded by him in the *Almagest* can be fixed between the years 127 and 151 C.E. Combining these facts with the Arabic tradition that has him living until the age of 78, Ptolemy's lifetime can be put between 100 and 178 C.E., or roughly a generation after Nicomachus.

4. Aristoxenus referred to these *harmoniai* or tunings as "species of the octave" (εἴδη τοῦ διὰ πασῶν). The forms in which he gave them are preserved by the chief Aristoxenian theorist of antiquity, Cleonides, in his *Introduction to Harmonics* 9 (Jan 197.4–198.13). Each is an octave segment of the Greater Perfect System: Mixolydian (B–B), Lydian (C–C), Phrygian (D–D), Dorian (E–E), Hypolydian (F–F), Hypophrygian (G–G), Hypodorian (A–A¹).

5. Nicomachus' highest tetrachord—hyperbolaion—must admit an E♭ in order to comply with the laws of tetrachordal form: semi-tone, whole-tone, whole-tone.

6. Pachymeres, *Harm.* 11 (Tannery, 127.10–12). Cf. Barker, II (1989), p. 264, n. 80. Chailley (1956), 92–93 attempted to show that Nicomachus' system is in reality the usual fourteen note system if one considers the seventh note from either end to be not the same note (A), but two different notes (A and B). Chailley's interpretation is as follows:

$$1 \quad 2 \quad 3 \quad 4 \quad 5 \quad 6 \quad 7 \quad 7 \quad 6 \quad 5 \quad 4 \quad 3 \quad 2 \quad 1$$
si do re mi fa sol la si do re mi fa sol la

7. Ps.-Plutarch, *De mus.* ch. 30; 1141D–1142A. On this celebrated fragment, see Comotti, pp. 127–28, who suggests that Phrynis' "screwball" (*strobilos*) "was probably a sort of *capotasto*, a device for changing the tuning of the cithara" (p. 127).

8. Plato, *Rep.* 399C7–D.

9. Cf. Levin (1961), 295–96.

10. Pausanias 3.12.8.

11. See note 10 above. Cf. Henderson (1957), 397, who argues that the stories about Timotheos' addition of new strings to the lyre are in the main apocryphal.

12. The pentachord is encompassed by hypate meson (E) at the lower extreme and by paramese (B) at the upper extreme.

13. No account of the Greater Perfect System is found in the writings of Aristoxenus, nor is there any trace of it in his extant work. All such information must be learned from Cleonides, *Intro. Harm.* 4 (Jan, 182.5–22), and Euclid, *Sectio Canonis* (Jan, 166). According to Plutarch, *De an. Proc. in Timaeo* 1029C, the addition of proslambanomenos was accomplished by "the moderns," that is, in relatively recent times. The material is reviewed by Boethius, *De inst. mus.* 1.20 (Friedlein, 211.21–212.7), who names his source (Friedlein, 205.27) as Nicomachus. As Bower, p. 29 n. 96, points out, this material must come from Nicomachus' promised longer work on music.

14. For the Greeks, the guiding degree is mese (A) and the paradigmatic scale formed in relation to mese has the same structure as the modern key of A natural minor (i.e., minus the $G_\sharp$). This paradigmatic scale was the ancient hypodorian. Cf. Chailley (1979), p. 79. Within the framework of this scale there is comprehended the eleven note system of an octave and a fourth comprising the three tetrachords hypaton, meson, and synemmenon. This was called the Lesser Perfect System or Σύστημα τέλειον ἔλαττον. It was also thought of as the "System of Synemmenon," as in Ptolemy, *Harm.* 2.6 (Düring, 54.2).

15. A *pyknon* is the sum of the two quarter-tones in the enharmonic tetrachord. It is also applied to the sum of the two semi-tones of the chromatic tetrachord. A *katapyknosis* is a diagram in which all these small intervals are listed at the same time. Aristoxenus, *Harm. El.* 1.28 (Da Rios, 36.1–6) has this to say of such an enterprise: "In inquiring into continuity we must avoid the example set by the Harmonists in their condensed diagrams (*katapyknoseis*), where they mark as consecutive notes those that are separated from one another by the smallest interval. For so far is the voice from being able to produce twenty-eight consecutive dieses that it can by no effort produce three dieses in succession" (tr. Macran). Indeed, Aristoxenus might well have been commenting on Nicomachus' procedure in

Excerpt 9.

16. Cf. Introduction, p. 26, n. 34.

17. See Heath, II (1921), pp. 106–07.

18. Thrasyllus' division of the canon is reported by Theon (Hiller, 87.9–93.7). See R. and D. Lawlor, p. 59.

19. On Eratosthenes' *Platonicus*, see Heath, II (1921), pp. 104–05. On the *Platonicus* as a source for Nicomachus, see D'Ooge, p. 27.

20. On the question of Nicomachus' criticism of Thrasyllus and Eratosthenes, see Barker, II (1989), p. 266, n. 87.

21. Plato, *Tim.* 20A1–5.

22. For the history of this treatise, see Taylor, pp. 655–64. Cf. Levin (1975), p. 92, n. 93 for additional references. This passage in the *Manual* is generally accepted as the first reference in the literature to the treatise, and, therefore, is considered to be a *terminus ante quem*. It is an important factor in dating the treatise somewhere between 20 B.C.E. and 120 C.E. See Taylor, pp. 656–57 for the evidence on dating the treatise.

23. This is reported by Aulus Gellius, *Noctes Atticae* 3.17: "For many pieces of silver you procured a little book, and starting from it, you learned to write the *Timaeus.*"

24. Diogenes Laertius, 8.84–85.

25. See Taylor, pp. 142–43.

26. [Iamblichus] *Theologoumena Arithmeticae* (De Falco, 46.25–47.2). Cf. Waterfield, p. 78.

Chapter 12

On the progression and division of the notes in the three genera

IN ORDER that you may have the progression in the three genera from proslambanomenos up to hyperbolaion nete in an orderly extension, it is suitable that I recapitulate for the sake of clarity, beginning with the statements I made a little earlier.

A note is an indivisible vocal utterance, an auditory monad, as it were. But as the moderns say, it is the incidence of the voice upon a single and simple point of pitch. While, according to some, it is a sound without breadth and without intervals in its region.

An interval is the intervening space between two notes. Relationship, however, is the ratio which measures the distance in each interval; and difference is the excess or deficiency of the notes compared with one another. Those who believe that difference and relationship are the same thing are wrong in their thinking. For consider: 2 to 1 comprises the same difference as 1 does to 2 but not the same relationship. For 2 is twice that of 1, but 1 is half of 2. And further, among all the terms of an arithmetic mean, whether they be three or even more, the difference is the same among all, but the relationship is of one sort or another. But you will be provided with more copious information on this question in my extensive treatment of the subject.

A system is a combination of two or more intervals. But no note among the intervals is consonant with the one immediately following it, but is completely dissonant with it. Among the systems, however, some are consonant, others dissonant. Systems are consonant when the notes comprising them, though they be different in compass, commingle with one another when played together or are somehow sounded simultaneously, in such a way that the sound produced from them is of a oneness like a single voice. Notes are dissonant, however, when the sound emanating from both of them is heard to be disparate in some way and unblended.

Since the first and most elementary consonance is the fourth in a continuous tetrachord in epitritic [4:3] proportion, it is reasonable to find in this tetrachord the variations from one to another of the three genera of melody. For the diatonic, about which we spoke earlier, progresses in this way: semi-tone, then a whole-tone, then a whole-tone—three intervals within four numbers, that is to say, within four notes. For this reason it is called "diatonic," from the fact that it is the only one of the rest of the genera that progresses "by tones." The chromatic progresses in this way: semi-tone, then another semi-tone, then after these, an incomposite trihemitone. And this genus is disposed in such a way that even if it is not composed outright of two whole-tones and a semi-tone, it may be observed, nevertheless, to comprise intervals that are equivalent to two whole-tones and a semi-tone. The enharmonic comprehends by nature such a progression as the following: quarter-tone, which is half of a semi-tone, another quarter-tone, the sum of both being equal to a semi-tone, and the remaining interval of the tetrachord, an entire incomposite ditone. And this is distributed in such a way that it is also equivalent to two whole-tones and a semi-tone; for within these intervals it is impossible for one note to be consonant with another.

It is evident, therefore, that the variations of the genera do not assume their difference within the four notes of the tetrachord, but within the two middle notes only. In the chromatic, therefore, the third note was altered in relation to the diatonic, but the second remained the same as in the diatonic and at the same pitch as the third note in the enharmonic. In the enharmonic the two middle notes were altered in relation to the diatonic in such a way that the enharmonic is opposite to the diatonic, and the chromatic is between these two, for it deviates minimally from the diatonic, by one semi-tone only. From whence we say that men who are changeable have "color."

The extreme notes of the tetrachord, then, are called "fixed notes," for they do not deviate in any of the genera; while the middle notes are "movables," at least in the enharmonic. In the chromatic, however, the second note is both movable and immovable, for relative to the diatonic it does not vary, but relative to the enharmonic it does vary.

The octave, being a system distributed over eight strings, whether

one reckons downwards from mese to proslambanomenos or up-
wards from mese to nete hyperbolaion—amounting to a fourth
which consists of two whole-tones and a semi-tone and a fifth
which consists of three whole-tones and a semi-tone—does not
consist of six whole-tones exactly, as the moderns believe, but of
five whole-tones and two semi-tones so-called. If these semi-tones
were really halves of whole-tones, what would prevent a whole-
tone from being composed of them and the octave from consisting
of six whole-tones? We shall offer a clear and very detailed explanation of this problem in our extensive treatment of the subject.
Indeed, Philolaus agrees with us in the preceding citation in which
he says, "A *harmonia* consists of five sesquioctaves and two
dieseis," that is, two semi-tones, which would make one whole-
tone if they were truly halves of whole-tones.

Accordingly, the names of the three genera amalgamated with
one another in the same diagram will be these:*

proslambanomenos ....A₁
hypate hypaton ....B₁
parhypate hypaton enharmonic ....B₁+
parhypate hypaton chromatic and diatonic.................C
enharmonic hypaton..C
chromatic hypaton..C♯
diatonos hypaton ....D
hypate meson ....E
parhypate meson enharmonic ....E+
parhypate meson chromatic and diatonic ....F
meson enharmonic ....F
meson chromatic ....F♯
meson diatonic...G
mese...A
trite synemmenon enharmonic ....A+
trite synemmenon chromatic and diatonic ....B♭

* The sign + indicates the rise of a quarter-tone.

synemmenon enharmonic .... B♭

synemmenon chromatic .... B

synemmenon diatonic .... C'

nete synemmenon .... D'

paramese .... B'

trite diezeugmenon enharmonic .... B'+

trite diezeugmenon chromatic and diatonic .... C'

enharmonic diezeugmenon .... C'

chromatic diezeugmenon .... C'♯

diatonic diezeugmenon .... D'

nete diezeugmenon .... E'

trite hyperbolaion enharmonic .... E'+

trite hyperbolaion chromatic and diatonic .... F'

enharmonic hyperbolaion .... F'

chromatic hyperbolaion .... F'♯

diatonic hyperbolaion .... G'

nete hyperbolaion .... A'

Please forgive the haste of such writing as this—for you are aware that you asked me while I was completely unsettled in transit—and, consistent with your most gentle and altogether most intelligent nature, please accept this as first fruits of a sort and friendship's offering. And if the gods be willing, please await my treatise which will be a very copious and complete discourse on the subject discussed here. I shall send it to you directly, as the earliest opportunity presents itself.

Commentary 12

IN Chapter 4 Nicomachus defined the three elements of which music is composed: musical note, being a pitch without breadth; musical interval, being a distance between two notes of unequal pitch; and musical system, being a synthesis of more than one interval.[1] He then went on to explain the relation in which these three elements stood to mathematics. He showed, to begin with, that the factors productive of musical pitch and pitch difference—i.e. size of the sounding-body and speed of vibration—are quantitative, and hence measurable.[2] He then proceeded to demonstrate how these quantitative and measurable factors are governed by the mathematical laws of inverse proportion. In so doing he aimed to show that the contemplation of these musical elements is a legitimate intellectual pursuit, one that issued in genuine mathematical knowledge. Indeed, the knowledge which Nicomachus details throughout the *Manual* is, to this day, certain, exact, and applicable to the real world of acoustical phenomena. Moreover, as Nicomachus has been at pains to argue, this knowledge can be obtained by thought alone—that is, without the aid of observation. Thus, a single string under tension supplies the single pitch that ignites the entire mathematical apparatus by which all other pitches can be computed. And from that point on, pure thought can take charge. In sum, there is implicit in everything that Nicomachus has said thus far the notion that thought is superior to the ear in judging of the accuracy of things heard.[3] So that, if the testimony of the ear does not agree with the mathematics as detailed by Nicomachus, then so much the worse for the ear. This is the philosophy to which Nicomachus subscribed; it began, of course, with Pythagoras.

In this final chapter of the *Manual*, Nicomachus returns to the three musical elements that he had defined in Chapter 4; this time, however, with a far different purpose. For to judge by what he presents here (and promises to present in his longer work), Nicomachus seems intent on one thing: to describe the ways in which these three elements function in music. This required that he take into account their melodic background, an enterprise that

177

was partially anticipated in Chapter 2. There, he introduced
Aristoxenus' theory of vocal motion and vocal space—a theory
which he attributed most improperly to the Pythagoreans. Here, he
elaborates the basic structure of Aristoxenus' theory of music, from
the tetrachord up to a full *katapyknosis* of the three genera in the
Immutable System. In so doing, Nicomachus implicitly acknowl-
edges that the three elements—note, interval, and system—are
subject to laws of a distinctly non-mathematical nature—to laws,
instead, of a primarily musical sort. These, however—the laws of
Aristoxenus' theory of music—are, as he implied in the case of the
semi-tone, incompatible with the basic tenets of Pythagorean
harmonic science. Yet, as seems apparent in this chapter,
Nicomachus believed that he could nevertheless incorporate them
into the framework of Pythagorean harmonics. In this, he was far
more accommodating or, what may be the case, far more uncritical,
than Aristoxenus had been centuries earlier where the Pythagoreans
were concerned. Disdaining to mention them by name, this is what
Aristoxenus had to say of the Pythagoreans and their mathematical
theory:

> For some of them introduced extraneous reasoning and, rejecting
> the senses as inaccurate, fabricated rational principles, asserting
> that height and depth of pitch consist in certain numerical ratios
> and relative rates of vibration—a theory utterly extraneous to the
> subject and quite at variance with the phenomena (tr. Macran).[4]

Whereas Aristoxenus knew the tenets of Pythagorean harmonics
thoroughly enough to warrant his rejection of them on the grounds
he adduces in the above passage, Nicomachus, for his part, understood the teachings of Aristoxenus intimately enough to absorb
them, where need be, into his own discipline. To be sure,
Nicomachus was sufficiently Pythagorean to think that without
mathematics no true wisdom was possible. Yet, as he makes
evident in this chapter, Aristoxenus' influence on him was such as
to predispose him to favor certain characteristics of what is essentially a purely musical theory. These characteristics, speaking
broadly, were melodic motion and space (as in Chapter 2), melodic

progression (as in Chapter 7), and melodic function (*dynamis*), as in the present chapter.[5] It is from Aristoxenus, then, that he derives most of what he offers here: the definition of musical note, the function of musical notes in scales, the fixed and movable functions of musical notes in the formation of genera, and the locus of each note in the Immutable System.

Against this theoretical framework, Nicomachus, being the orthodox Pythagorean that he was, reminds the reader of certain fundamental conflicts between his own position on the elements of music and that of the Aristoxenians. Thus, where the measurement of intervals is the question at issue, he points out that intervals, being the difference between notes, are expressible only by mathematical ratios and not by differences between numbers.[6] So too, he pauses in his explanation long enough to mention the fact that octaves do not comprise six whole-tones, but five whole-tones—and two semi-tones, that semi-tones, so-called, are not really halves of whole-tones, as "the moderns" believe. For these, the beliefs of "the moderns" (by which term Nicomachus meant the Aristoxenians) were derived from the world of the senses, where nothing can be unchanging or trustworthy.

Something must have led Nicomachus to believe that between these two different approaches to the same phenomena there were grounds for reconciliation, that between mathematical knowledge—the object of the intellect—and the musical phenomena—the object of the ear—there were areas of compatibility. The question is, how was Nicomachus to retain his belief in the timeless and eternal reality of numbers, while admitting into his theory the shifting colorations and other-worldliness of Aristoxenus' musical abstractions? We will never know. What we do know is that Nicomachus intended to face such problems; unfortunately, along with his lost longer work on music, any of his efforts to this end are also lost.

Pythagorean influence may be occasionally discerned in the observations that Nicomachus offers on the measurement of intervals, the indivisibility of the whole-tone, and the structure of the octave; on the whole, however, what Nicomachus presents here is a rapid course on the fundamentals of Aristoxenus' theory of music.

He begins with his own arithmologically-oriented definition of a musical note as an "atomic" or indivisible element, an element which he likens to the "monad." In another work he says of the monad that it "is the beginning, middle, and end of quantity, of size and, moreover, of quality," and he adds that to the Pythagoreans it was the source of all things, embodying, among other things, "being," "order," and "concord."[7] In thus stressing the fundamental and unitary character of the monad, the position of Nicomachus is perfectly consistent with that of the Aristoxenians. Indeed, their definition of the musical note, as he reports it, is that of Aristoxenus himself: "It is the incidence of the voice on one point of pitch."[8] According to Aristoxenus, theoreticians such as Lasus of Hermione and certain members of the school of Epigonus had been misguided in assigning a "breadth" or extension to musical notes.[9] On the contrary, in holding that a musical note is a sound without extension and without any spaces or parts in its composition, that, like the monad, it is one with itself, Nicomachus is in complete agreement with Aristoxenus.

Nicomachus has three comments to make about intervals. Two of them are derived from Aristoxenus, while the third is essentially a Pythagorean digression. First, Nicomachus' definition of an interval as a space intervening between two notes comes from Aristoxenus, but with this difference: that of Aristoxenus is more specific, running as follows: "An interval is the space bounded by two notes that do not have the same pitch."[10] Nicomachus' second point of agreement where intervals are concerned is contained in his statement about "difference" (*diaphora*). Difference, he says, is the excess or deficiency of notes compared with one another. Aristoxenus puts it this way: "An interval is a difference between points of pitch."[11] As an example of this kind of difference, Aristoxenus refers to a whole-tone as the difference between a fifth and a fourth.[12]

Nicomachus next adds to his Aristoxenian statements the observation that the difference between the terms of the ratio that measures an interval is not the same thing as the meaning or signification of that ratio.[13] So that the ratio in his example—2:1—is that which measures the octave, and it signifies a duple relation (*schesis*). But this signification has nothing at all to do with the difference that exists between the terms of the ratio, which difference in this case (that of the octave ratio) is one, or one-half of two. Extending this digression a little further, Nicomachus goes on to explain that in an arithmetic series, as for example 6, 9, 12, the difference between the terms is the same, namely, 3; but the relationship between the terms is not the same. On the contrary, the relation of 9 to 6 and of 9 to 12 is one of inequality, in that the ratio expressing these relations is on the one hand hemiolic (3:2) and, on the other, epitritic (3:4). Aristoxenus' response to this type of analysis can be imagined. He would have agreed to the truth contained in the numbers themselves, but he would have questioned the relevance of such mathematical extrapolations to the question of musical intervals and their differences.

Nicomachus' definition of *systema*, or scale, comes directly from Aristoxenus, who put it: "A system is to be regarded as the combination of two or more intervals";[14] that is to say, a scale can be composed of more than two intervals, but not of less than two. Nicomachus' observation as to the internal composition of any systematic arrangement of intervals, i.e. that "the successive notes in a scale are discordant with one another," would have been too self-evident for Aristoxenus to mention. In keeping with his general approach to the musical phenomena, he had arrived inductively at the principle that all intervals smaller than a fourth are discords, and this principle effectively comprehends those particulars that Nicomachus noticed in his statement.[15]

The criterion by which Nicomachus determines the consonance or dissonance of a system is based on that of Aristoxenus, who says:

> It is obvious that scales may differ both in compass and owing to the fact that the notes bounding that compass may be either concordant or discordant.[16]

In other words, a scale or system of intervals is considered to be concordant or discordant depending on the interval comprised by the extremes. The various possibilities are detailed by Aristoxenus and can be represented as follows:[17]

Concordant system:
  fourth + fifth = octave
  Sum of one or more octaves and a fourth
  Sum of one or more octaves and a fifth

Discordant system:
  fifth + fifth
  fourth + fourth
  octave + fifth + fifth
  octave + fourth + fourth

Nicomachus' criterion for judging the concordancy or discordancy of a musical interval is identity (a "oneness" [ἑνοειδές] as he calls it) or lack of identity, as this property is registered upon the ear. And, according to the unanimous opinion of all the theorists who dealt with the subject, the only intervals that met this criterion of concordancy were the fourth, the fifth, and the octave. In making the ear the final arbiter determining the concordancy or discordancy of a musical interval, Nicomachus would appear to be contradicting what for every Pythagorean was an article of faith, namely, that sensory evidence was theoretically inadmissible. Serving as a counterweight to this doctrinal waywardness, however, was the pivotal role played in the analysis by oneness, a Pythagorean concept of the highest significance. This mathematical concept was for Nicomachus of the same order of importance as the monad—the beginning of all things. Nicomachus' predilection toward Pythagorean doctrine is borne out by something that he wrote elsewhere, something that holds with the purely Pythagorean view concerning musical intervals: that the simpler the numerical ratio involved in the expression of a musical interval, the more perfect is the concord. Thus, Nicomachus *apud* Boethius:

> It is not a single vibration which produces a uniform sound; but the string, once set into motion, gives rise to numerous sounds, since it imparts to the air numerous vibrations. However, when

the rapidity of these impacts upon the air is so great that one sound is mixed in some such way with another, one does not perceive the distance which separates them, and that is why we say it is a oneness of sound that reaches our ears.[18]

This may be one of the earliest references to the Pythagorean discovery that consonance is associated with the smallest of numbers. Above all, the implication here is that concordancy depends on one's response to the ratios rather than to the sounds themselves. In short, the farther one goes from the number one, the more discordant is the interval. This may be represented as follows:

Interval	Ratio	Largest number
unison	1:1	1
octave	2:1	2
fifth	3:2	3
fourth	4:3	4
major third	5:4	5
major sixth	5:3	5
minor third	6:5	6
minor sixth	8:5	8
whole-tone	9:8	9
semi-tone	256:245	256

Figure 7. Table of Intervals

The remarkable fact disclosed here is that the interval in which the two notes are farthest apart on the line of pitch turns out to be that which most closely approaches Nicomachus' "oneness"—i.e., the octave in duple ratio.[19]

Before setting out for his reader the Immutable System in all three genera, Nicomachus gives her a rapid course in the genera, explaining that the variation in each generic progression affects only the movable or interior notes of the tetrachord. The outer notes remain fixed on the same pitch, however, no matter how great the variation of the movable notes. Accordingly, he outlines the progression in each genus in such a way that his reader can compare the positions of each note:[20]

GENUS	FIXED	MOVABLE	MOVABLE	FIXED
	hypate meson	lichanos meson	parhypate meson	mese
DIATONIC:	E	F	G	A
		semi-tone	whole-tone	whole-tone	
CHROMATIC:	E	F	G♭	A
		semi-tone	semi-tone	trihemitone	
ENHARMONIC:	E	E+	F	A
		quarter-tone	quarter-tone	ditone	

Figure 8. The Three Genera

Finally, Nicomachus reminds his reader that the octave, reckoning from mese (A) down to proslambanomenos (A₁), or from mese (A) up to nete hyperbolaion (A¹), is not really equivalent to six whole-tones (as the Aristoxenians think), but rather to five whole-tones and two semi-tones, which are not really halves of whole-tones. Referring her to the Philolaic passage of Chapter 9, Nicomachus promises to enlarge on these matters sometime in the future. And before bidding her farewell for the present, he affixes to his epistolary treatise a tabulation of the twenty-eight different pitches that are also to be found in *Excerpt* 8.[21] Begging her forbearance in the most appropriate (if indeed in the most difficult to translate terms),[22] Nicomachus continues on his way, enduring all the ills of the second century C.E. traveler.

Notes to Chapter 12

1. Aristoxenus, the first to arrive at the definition of these three elements, asks the reader's indulgence because, as he says, *Harm. El.* 1.16 (Da Rios, 21.13–16): "it is perhaps difficult in the case of all things that are elementary to the subject to give an account of them that embraces an exhaustive and accurate interpretation, and this is not least so in the case of note, interval, and scale."

2. See above, Chapter 4 commentary, p. 67.

3. Thus Glaukon in Plato's *Rep.* 531B1 observes of the empirical musicians, who cannot agree on the size of a particular interval: "They prefer to use their ears rather than their minds."

4. Aristoxenus, *Harm. El.* 2.32 (Da Rios, 41.17–42.3).

5. As explained in the commentary to Chapter 8, pp. 111–12, the function of a pitch is determined by the laws of musical logic. Thus any progression of notes is determined with reference to the "fixed" or "movable" function—*dynamis*—of the pitches in the scale. This notion of *dynamis* is central to Aristoxenus' theory of music. Cf. Levin (1972), 226–29.

6. Interestingly enough, however, it was on the basis of the arithmetic difference between the terms of the ratio 243:216 and 216:192, or 27 and 24, that Philolaus computed the size of the small semi-tone, or *diesis*, of 13 units (which is also the difference between Plato's ratio for the semi-tone 256:243) and the *apotome* of 14 units. As explained above (pp. 135–36), the difference between these terms (=1) he called *comma*, and half a *comma* he called *schisma*. This is, in fact, Nicomachus' own method for computing intervals in *Excerpt 2*.

7. [Iamblichus] *Theologoumena Arithmeticae* (De Falco, 3.7–8; De Falco, 6.5–9). Cf. Waterfield, pp. 35ff.

8. Aristoxenus, *Harm. El.* 1.15 (Da Rios, 20.16–17).

9. Aristoxenus, *Harm. El.* 1.3 (Da Rios, 7.19–22).

10. Aristoxenus, *Harm. El.* 1.15 (Da Rios, 20.20–21.1).

11. Aristoxenus, *Harm. El.* 1.15 (Da Rios, 21.1–2).

12. Aristoxenus, *Harm. El.* 1.21 (Da Rios, 27.14–16).

13. Cf. above, n. 6. See also, Barker, II (1989), p. 267, n. 92.

14. Aristoxenus, *Harm. El.* 1.16 (Da Rios, 21.6–7).

15. Aristoxenus, *Harm. El.* 2.45 (Da Rios, 56.1–5).

16. Aristoxenus, *Harm. El.* 1.17 (Da Rios, 22.5–7).

17. Aristoxenus, *Harm. El.* 2.45 (Da Rios, 56.10–19). As Aristoxenus points out here, the property that is peculiar to the octave is that if it is added to any concord, the end result is a concord. But doubling the smaller concords—fifths and fourths—produces a discord even when the octave is added to such compounds.

18. Boethius, *De inst. mus.* 1.3 (Friedlein, 190.13).

19. Thus Jeans, p. 154 asks: "'Why is consonance associated with the ratios of small numbers?' And although many attempts have been made to answer it, the question is not fully answered yet."

20. Cf. Chapter 7 where Nicomachus analyzes the tetrachordal progressions in the diatonic genus. Using as his frame of reference the diatonic, Nicomachus finds that the enharmonic, when compared with it, shows the greatest variation, and in this sense is "opposite" to the diatonic; the chromatic varies in a lesser degree from the diatonic, thus occupying, according to Nicomachus, an intermediate position between the diatonic and the enharmonic. Because the alteration from diatonic to chromatic requires only one change, this being the lowering of lichanos (G) by one semi-tone only, Nicomachus remarks that the chromatic diverges only slightly from the diatonic. By comparing this alteration of the diatonic with that of the individuals who are "easily turned" (εὐτρέπτους), he means to emphasize the facility with which a musician can produce the subtle but unmistakable change from the diatonic to the chromatic genus. On this topic, Aristoxenus has this to say (*Harm. El.* 1.19; Da Rios 24.20–25.4): "Of these genera the diatonic must be granted to be the first and oldest, inasmuch as mankind lights upon it before the others; the chromatic comes next. The enharmonic is the third and most recent; and it is only at a late stage, and with great labor and difficulty that the ear becomes accustomed to it" (tr. Macran).

21. For Aristoxenus' opinion of this sort of enterprise, see Chapter 11 above, n. 15.

22. On the difficulty of this passage, see Barker, II (1989), p. 269, n. 102. As Meibom has it, p. 28: nosti enim, quod in ipso itinere faciendo mihi animi omnino suspenso hoc mandaris, secundum morem tuum mitissimum et ubique prudentissimum.

Appendix:

Excerpts from Nicomachus

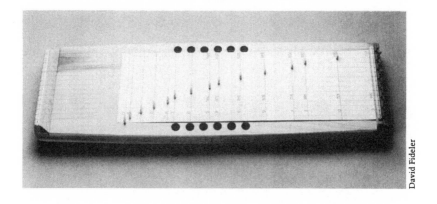

Figure 9. A Fifteen-stringed Monochord or Polychord

This polychord with fifteen strings is described by Ptolemy in his treatise *On Harmonics*, book 3, chapter 1. It allows the researcher to set up a double-octave system, the Greek Greater Perfect System, two different tuning systems side-by-side, and so forth.

In the photograph above is shown the regular diatonic scale described in Plato's *Timaeus*, spanning two octaves. In order to set up this scale on the polychord, the length of the *canon* needs to be divided into 972 parts. In the table below, both string divisions and the tone-numbers are expressed in the lowest possible whole-number terms:

String divisions (Length)	Tone numbers (Vibration)	Tones (in key of C)	Intervals between tones
486	768	C	
			leimma (256:243)
512	729	B	
			whole-tone (9:8)
576	648	A	
			whole-tone (9:8)
648	576	G	
			whole-tone (9:8)
729	512	F	
			leimma (256:243)
768	486	E	
			whole-tone (9:8)
864	432	D	
			whole-tone (9:8)
972	384	C	

Excerpts from Nicomachus

1. They say that Hermes invented the lyre from the tortoise-shell, and providing it with seven strings, handed down the art of lyre-playing to Orpheus. And Orpheus taught Thamyris and Linus. Linus taught Heracles, by whom he was killed. He also taught Amphion, the Theban, who built Thebes with seven gates after the seven strings of the lyre. When Orpheus was killed by the Thracian women, his lyre was thrown into the sea and was cast up in the city of Antissa in Lesbos. Fishermen found it and carried it to Terpander and he took it to Egypt. The story goes that he discovered it and then brought it to perfection and demonstrated it to the priests in Egypt, alleging that he was the first to invent it. Thus it is said that Terpander invented the lyre, and the Achaeans inherited it from Cadmus the son of Agenor. Such are the current reports.

2. There are numbers from which musicians form intervals consisting of whole-tones. In the case of the fourth, which they say is observed to be in the epitritic [4:3] proportion, consisting of two whole-tones and a certain fraction, as, for example, when it begins with parhypate hypaton and ends with parhypate meson; they take as an epitritic number—256 to 192—and, starting from this 192, they take it through the sesquioctave ratios in which the intervals of a whole-tone are computed (the *leimma* being left over), they complete the number 256. Accordingly, then, they raise the interval a whole-tone starting from 192 and arrive at 216 which is the sesquioctave of 192; for it contains 192 and its eighth, 24. Again, starting from 216, they raise it a whole-tone and arrive at 243 which is the sesquioctave of 216; for it contains it and its eighth, 27. To arrive at the completion of the fourth and of the number 256, there remains the number 13 which is neither half of the first whole-tone, calculated in terms of the number 24, nor is it half of the second whole-tone, calculated in terms of the number 27.

In the case of the fifth, which is organized in a hemiolic [3:2] proportion and is composed of three whole-tones and a certain fraction, as, for example, when it begins with parhypate meson and

189

ends with trite diezeugmenon, they deal with the question at issue in the following way. They take as a hemiolic number—768 to 512—and, starting from this 512, they take it through the sesquioctave [9:8] ratios in which the intervals of a whole-tone are computed and, with the left-over *leimma*, they complete the number 768. Accordingly, then, they raise the interval a whole-tone starting from 512 and arrive at 576, which is the sesquioctave of 512; for it contains the number 512 itself and its eighth, 64. Again, starting from 576, they raise the interval a whole-tone and arrive at 648, a sesquioctave of 576, since it contains this number, 576, and its eighth, 72. Again, starting from 648, they raise the interval a whole-tone and arrive at its sesquioctave, 729, which is the sesquioctave of 648 since it contains it and and the number 81, which is an eighth of 648. To complete the hemiolic number, 768, there is left remaining, the number 39. But 39 is neither half of 64, in terms of which the first whole-tone is calculated, nor is it half of 72, in terms of which the second whole-tone is calculated, nor is it half of 81, in terms of which is the third whole-tone calculated. For the whole-tone is not exactly divided into two semi-tones.

And yet it is also true in the case of the fourth consisting of a whole-tone and a leimma and a whole-tone, as, for example, when one starts with proslambanomenos and ends with diatone hypaton, in which case they deal with it in this way. Again, they take as an epitritic number, 288 to 216. And starting with 216, they raise the interval a whole-tone and arrive at 243, which is a sesquioctave of 216 and exceeds 216 by 27. But since we cannot raise the interval a whole-tone starting with 243, for we do not find it to be a complete sesquioctave, we achieve, by lowering it a whole-tone, the sesquioctave's reciprocal of 288. The reciprocal sesquioctave of 288 is 256 because it is contained wholly by 288 plus its eighth, 32. The result of raising the interval starting with 216 through the sesquioctave ratio of a whole-tone, 243 is found; while the result of lowering the interval starting with 288 through the sesquioctave ratio of a whole-tone, 256 is found. But in order that the entire intermediary number be completed, there is left remaining the number 13, which is neither half of 27 nor is it half of 32. Taken in another way, the entire system of a fourth is, in terms of the aforementioned numbers, 72. But in terms of the sesquioctave obtained by raising the interval, the number 27 will be found; while in terms of the sesquioctave obtained by lowering the interval, the number 32 will be found. And if we subtract from 72 the numbers 27 and 32, there is left remaining the number 13, which is neither half of 27 nor of 32.

Again, in the case of the fifth which is constituted of a whole-tone and a *leimma* and two whole-tones, as, for example, when one starts with diatone hypaton and ends with mese, they offer the following arrangement. They take as a hemiolic number, 1296 to 864, and starting with this, the 864, they raise the interval a whole-tone and arrive at 972, which is greater than 864 by 108. But since we cannot raise the interval a whole-tone starting with 972, we find it by lowering the interval. Accordingly, we lower it starting with 1296 and we find the number 1152, which is the reciprocal sesquioctave of 1296 and is exceeded by 1296 by the number 144, which is an eighth of 1152. Again, we lower the interval accordingly starting with 1152 and we find the number 1024, which is the reciprocal sesquioctave of 1152 and is exceeded by 1152 by the number 128, which is an eighth of 1024. Therefore, from 1024 to 972, the point at which the whole-tone is fixed when one raises the interval starting with 864, there is left remaining the number 52. This number is not a half of any of those numbers which were discovered among the whole-tones; it is not half of 108, nor of 128, nor of 144; for it is among these numbers that the whole-tone intervals are found.

3. [Nicomachus says] that in the distribution of the notes of the heptachord the topmost and first string is called hypate. This is indeed because Kronos is the highest and the first reckoning from the sphere of the fixed stars; the lowest is called neate after Selene since it is the most remote sphere of them all, while the middle string is called mese after Helios. Of the strings on either side of nete and hypate, the one next to hypate is called parhypate after Zeus, while the other one next to nete is called paranete not after Hermes, but unconventionally after Aphrodite, unless there is a mistake in the written account; and hypermese is named after Ares,

and trite after Aphrodite. The highest note belongs to Selene, if she assumes the position of nete, while the low note belongs to Kronos, if he assumes the position of hypate.

Those who first began to reckon from the spheres nearest to us say, however, that hypate is the first note and belongs to Selene, since it is the beginning of the notes [of the scale], and that nete, since it is the farthest from us, belongs to Kronos. For the hypate is more related to terrestrial things, because in a multiple substance the power is weaker; so that because of its earthliness it embodies multiplicity and because of its multiplicity it is weak. For the power of all existing things lies in the fact that each is an entity unto itself. It is for this reason that the hypate was allocated to Selene since Selene is herself variable and changeable and has less power because of her greater distance from the sphere of fixed stars; and in this respect there is a certain fixed position of the heavenly bodies relative to her, just as there is among the notes ranging from nete to the hypate which do not admit of another consubstantial kind of distribution extending any further. For this reason hypate is allocated to Selene. For Selene is the first celestial body we encounter since she is nearer to the Earth. Indeed the low note has its origin in the lowest hollow parts of the body near the flanks, while the high note originates in the ears and the brain and the temple, which are the highest parts of the body. Neate is, therefore, the note of Kronos, because he is not susceptible of addition and because he embraces the other [celestial bodies] in his essence and his power. Accordingly then, because of the fact that the one, Selene, is slow and the other, Kronos, is fast in the movement of the cosmos in the same direction, and because of her lagging behind the planets, Selene is identified with the note, hypate. For Kronos is nearest to the sphere of fixed stars, lacking only one thirtieth of a degree, so that in the uniform motion [of the heavens] he lacks two minutes a day from the complete revolution of the universe, that is, one thirtieth of a degree. If we examine Selene in her uniform and daily movement, it is possibile to discover that she falls behind by thirteen degrees and fourteen minutes, so that it is reasonable to consider the one, Kronos, to be the swiftest of all the heavenly bodies and the other, Selene, the slowest.

4. [Nicomachus says] that all those who added other strings to the eight-stringed lyre were induced to do so not by any mathematical logic, but for the gratification of their listeners. Thus, Prophrastus the Pierian added the ninth string, Histiaeus of Colophon the tenth, and Timotheus the Milesian the eleventh, and others added the rest in sequence. Thereafter, the number of strings was brought by them to eighteen. And so Pherecrates, the comic poet, is observed to have censured the practice in his play entitled *Cheiron* for its debauchery of melodies.

In all, then, the strings in the three genera [or even more] amount to a total number of twenty-eight. There are neither more nor less than these owing to the fact that the human voice does not admit of sounds lower than these in the bass; for sounds uttered below these are booming and husky, indistinct intonations that are unarticulated and unmelodious. Sounds uttered above these in the treble screech like the cuckoo, the notes being very like the howling of wolves, and are unintelligible and incapable of participation in a consonance. The number of strings in each genus according as two middle notes are formed in the disjunctions [of tetrachords] so that a tetrachord may be consonant with a pentachord by disjunction—are eighteen. But those notes in the Immutable System which form no more than one middle note, but employ it as the lowest of the higher pitches and the highest of the lower pitches, are limited to fifteen strings for the double octave in the Immutable System. Indeed, Ptolemy agrees with this and says that we must remain fixed with this number, asserting that the tonoi are equal in number to the species of the octave (and to the species) of the fourth and of the fifth; and that it is from these tonoi that every note comprehends its homophone within this number of notes; and that the mese is exactly a middle note and that both extremes are limited, the bass to the proslambanomenos, the treble to the nete hyperbolaion.

5. [Nicomachus says] that since some carried the number of the notes up to twenty-eight, they will be seen not to have fallen outside of the consonance of the universe, but have followed the natural philosophy of Pythagoras and the doctrine of Plato. For the

nature of the divine souls is cut up by the twenty-seventh multiple, the monad, the origin of all things, being taken in addition (just as in the case of musical notes, they call the added note proslambanomenos) and amounts to so great a number; it starts with the seven terms which Plato postulated, and ends with the triple and cubic progressions which he discovered.

6. What is more, the notes of each of the seven spheres produce by nature a single kind of sound; to each of which the elementary speech sounds called vowels are referred. These individually and anything composed of them are not to be spoken aloud by the wise. Wherefore the note has the same power as the monad has in arithmetic and the point has in geometry. These elements are combined with material substances (as, for example, vowels are combined with consonants), just as the soul is combined with the body and *harmonia* is combined with the strings. When the soul is combined with the body, it produces living things; when *harmonia* is combined with the strings, it produces keys and melodies, these combinations being the active and consummating productions of the gods. Wherefore, whenever the initiates pay reverence to such an act, they invoke it symbolically with sigmas and clickings and inarticulate and meaningless sounds. [He says] that those who instituted the heptachord as a natural concord took it from this source; that such a construction comes not from the spheres, but from the sounds themselves that are inserted and interposed in every word, and that these sounds are the only ones among the letters that we call vowels and voiced utterances. But since the distribution of these sounds is simple, it is not adequate to designate anything complex, but there is required for the completion of a whole complex the combination and interconnection of one element with another, just as in the case of the lyre strings. It is in this way that the hebdomad is connected with the tetrad and the monad, as we said in our work on the *Hebdomad*. Therefore, the hebdomad multiplied by the tetrad in a cycle from the first term to the last and back again whether by addition or by subtraction amounts to such a number. For that is also true in the case of the spheres. It is evident how proportionately it is in the case of the

souls containing the spheres and conducting them around in an
orderly motion, each one conducting a separate sphere, according
to their increment, the sound belonging to each being added; but in
rhythm and position each of the others is lacking in number,
whence the circuit of sounds is said to be twenty-eight in number
according to the convention of the Egyptians.

7. Starting with these facts, Pythagoras discovered that the first
division and extension of the soul is limited to this number. For
indeed the soul is threefold, getting her substance from the Same,
and the Other, and from Being; and like substance, her tripartition
is limited to the rational, and the irrational, and the physical (just
as melodies are limited to the enharmonic, and the diatonic, and
the chromatic). And thence appears the bipartite division in the
Psychogonia itself which, in the seven notes, gives to the planets
the constitution of twenty-eight physical and spiritual notes that
is harmonious in essence; and to the sphere of the fixed stars, since
it is of the nature of the Same, and as it embraces the planets in
motion, it thus gives the cubic increment in the other number, 36,
which number is perfect and contains the augment of the right-
angled triangle the two sides of which are opposite to the hypotenuse. Perfected with the origin of all things, thence comes the first
tetraktys containing the source of the consonances which appears
in the numbers, 6, 8, 9, 12, and embraces the ratio of hypate and
mese, and nete and paramese, and the sesquioctave. For hypate has
reference to the number 6, mese to 8, nete to 12 and paramese to 9.
The sesquioctave is first observed in the ratio 8:9. This system
when condensed by quarter-tone intervals advances to that number
in which the degrees of the zodiac and the circuit of the zodiac is
limited.

8. But how, he says, are there said to be seven notes when there
are eight spheres? It is because the sphere [of fixed stars] that always
moves at the same rate produces a single and unvarying emission
of sound; and since it has no other sphere of a speed equal to it or
nearly equal, it can have no place in an attunement. [Whereas
among the first two planets, such is the case, since they are neither

equal nor unvarying]. But among the planets there are some that are shown to have a great dissimilarity and contrariness to it, having a movement as great as that of the Same is to that of the Other. That is why they let the note emitted by it be unmentioned.

9. The notes which are employed by the professional artists are these twenty-eight:

1. Proslambanomenos
2. Hypate hypaton
3. Parhypate hypaton
4. Hypaton enharmonic
5. Hypaton chromatic
6. Hypaton diatonic
7. Hypate meson
8. Parhypate meson
9. Meson enharmonic
10. Meson chromatic
11. Meson diatonic
12. Mese
13. Trite synemmenon
14. Paranete synemmenon enharmonic
15. Synemmenon chromatic
16. Synemmenon diatonic
17. Nete synemmenon
18. Paramesos
19. Trite diezeugmenon
20. Diezeugmenon enharmonic
21. Diezeugmenon chromatic
22. Diezeugmenon diatonic
23. Nete diezeugmenon
24. Trite hyperbolaion
25. Hyperbolaion enharmonic
26. Hyperbolaion chromatic
27. Hyperbolaion diatonic
28. Nete hyperbolaion

10. Just as some of the tetrachords in the three genera are hypaton, others are meson, others, synemmenon, others, diezeugmenon, and others are hyperbolaion, so it must be supposed that every spherical and divine being assumes something in the universe that has the relation in the attunement and constitution of the cosmos as of a beginning, something else as of a middle, and another as of an end—one thing being a conjunctive coagency, another a disjunctive one. And providence, using all these elements, produced a number that is divine, firm and unshaken and made the universe in melodic accord with itself, binding together every dominant and subordinate essence in such a proportion. Therefore, the first tetraktys, which is also the root of these tetrachords, is the cause in some way of all the divisions according to the genera, bringing about, as I have said, the number thirty-six belonging to the sphere of fixed stars, with the addition of the monad. And Plato, wishing to display this key of all the things that exist, in the thirteenth book of the *Nomoi*, when he had enumerated the last of all the explicative sciences, says, that it also apportioned to humans a consonant and symmetrical function.

Bibliography

Anderson, W. D. *Ethos and Education in Greek Music.* Cambridge: Harvard University Press, 1966.

Barker, A. *Greek Musical Writings: I. The Musician and his Art.* Cambridge: Cambridge University Press, 1984.

———. *Greek Musical Writings: II. Harmonic and Acoustic Theory.* Cambridge: Cambridge University Press, 1989.

Benade, A. H. *Horns, Strings, and Harmony.* Garden City: Doubleday, 1960.

Bower, Calvin M. *Fundamentals of Music. Anicius Manlius Severinus Boethius.* New Haven and London: Yale University Press, 1989.

Bowersock, G. W. *Greek Sophists in the Roman Empire.* Oxford: Clarendon Press, 1969.

Bragard, R. "L'harmonie des sphères selon Boèce," *Speculum* 4 (1929), 206–13.

Brumbaugh, R. L. *Plato's Mathematical Imagination: The Mathematical Passages in the Dialogues and their Interpretation.* Bloomington: Indiana University Press, 1954. Reprint. Millwood: Kraus Reprint Co., 1977.

Burkert, W. *Lore and Science in Ancient Pythagoreanism.* Translated by Edwin L. Minar, Jr. Cambridge: Harvard University Press, 1972.

Burnet, J. *Early Greek Philosophy.* 4th ed. New York: Meridian Books, 1957.

Chailley, J. "L'hexatonique grec d'après Nicomaque," *REG* 69 (1956), 73–100.

———. *La Musique Grecque Antique.* Paris: Société d'Édition "Les Belles Lettres," 1979.

Cherniss, H. *Aristotle's Criticism of Presocratic Philosophy.* Baltimore: The Johns Hopkins University Press, 1935. Reprint. New York: Octagon Books, 1971.

Comotti, Giovanni. *Music in Greek and Roman Culture.* Translated by Rosaria V. Munson. Baltimore and London: The Johns Hopkins University Press, 1989.

D'Ooge, M. L., Robbins, F. E. and Karpinski, L. C. *Nicomachus of Gerasa: Introduction to Arithmetic*. New York: Macmillan, 1926. Reprint. New York: Johnson Reprint Corporation, 1972.

Farmer, H. G. "The Music of Islam," *NOH*, pp. 421–464.

———. "The Music of Ancient Egypt," *NOH*, pp. 255–79.

Godwin, Joscelyn. *The Harmony of the Spheres: A Sourcebook of the Pythagorean Tradition in Music*. Rochester: Inner Traditions, 1993.

Guthrie, K. S. *The Pythagorean Sourcebook and Library: An Anthology of Ancient Writings which Relate to Pythagoras and Pythagorean Philosophy*. Grand Rapids: Phanes Press, 1988.

Guthrie, W. K. C. *A History of Greek Philosophy*. Vol. 1, *The Earlier Presocratics and the Pythagoreans*. Cambridge: Cambridge University Press, 1971.

Heath, Sir Thomas. *Aristarchus of Samos: The Ancient Copernicus*. Oxford: Clarendon Press, 1913.

———. *A History of Greek Mathematics*. Vol. 1, *From Thales to Euclid*. Vol. 2, *From Aristarchus to Diophantus*. Oxford: Clarendon Press, 1921.

Henderson, I. "Ancient Greek Music," *NOH*, pp. 336–403.

Howard, A. A. "The Aulos or Tibia," *HSCP* 4 (1893), 1–60.

Jeans, Sir J. *Science and Music*. Cambridge: Cambridge University Press, 1961.

Johnson, C. W. L. "The Motion of the Voice, ἡ τῆς φωνῆς κίνησις, in the Theory of Ancient Music," *TAPA* 30 (1899), 42–55.

Kline, M. *Mathematics in Western Culture*. Oxford: Oxford University Press, 1953.

Lasserre, Francois. *Plutarque de la musique*. Olten and Lausanne: Urs Graf-Verlag, 1954.

Lawlor, R. and D. *Mathematics Useful for Understanding Plato, by Theon of Smyrna, Platonic Philosopher*. San Diego: Wizards Bookshelf, 1979.

Levin, F. R. "The Hendecachord of Ion of Chios," *TAPA* 92 (1961), 295–307.

———. "Synesis in Aristoxenian Theory," *TAPA* 103 (1972), 211–34.

———. *The Harmonics of Nicomachus and the Pythagorean Tradition.* American Classical Studies, no. 1. University Park: The American Philological Association, 1975.

———. "πληγή and τάσις in the *Harmonika* of Klaudios Ptolemaios," *Hermes* 108 (1980), 205–29.

———. "Unity in Euclid's *Sectio Canonis,*" *Hermes* 118 (1990), 403–43

Maas, M. and Snyder, J. *Stringed Instruments of Ancient Greece.* New Haven and London: Yale University Press, 1989.

Macran, H. S. *The Harmonics of Aristoxenus.* Oxford: Clarendon Press, 1936.

Martin, Th. H. *Études sur le Timée de Platon, vol. I.* Paris: Société d'Édition"Les Belles Lettres," 1841.

McClain, E. G. *The Pythagorean Plato: Prelude to the Song Itself.* York Beach: Nicolas-Hays, 1978.

McDermott, W. C. "Plotina Augusta and Nicomachus of Gerasa," *Historia* 26 (1977), 192–203.

Meibom, M. *Antiquae Musicae Auctores Septem: Graece et Latine.* 2 vols. *Nicomachi Gerasseni Harmonices Manualis,* vol. 1, pp. 1–60. Amsterdam: L. Elzevier, 1652. Facsimile edition. New York: Broude Brothers Limited, 1977.

Merleau-Ponty, J. and Morando, B. *The Rebirth of Cosmology.* Translated by H. Weaver. Athens: Ohio University Press, 1982.

Michaelides, S. *The Music of Ancient Greece: An Encyclopedia.* London: Faber and Faber Limited, 1978.

Michel, P.-H. *De Pythagore à Euclide.* Paris: Société d'Édition "Les Belles Lettres," 1950.

Mountford, J. F. "Greek Music and its Relation to Modern Times," *JHS* (1920), 13–42.

Neugebauer, C. *The Exact Sciences in Antiquity.* New York: Dover, 1969.

Oxford Classical Dictionary. Edited by N. G. L. Hammond and H. H. Scullard. 2nd edition. Oxford: Clarendon Press, 1970.

Philip, J. A. *Pythagoras and Early Pythagoreanism.* Toronto: University of Toronto Press, 1966.

Ross, Sir D. *Aristotle's Physics: A Revised Text with Introduction and Commentary.* Oxford: Clarendon Press, 1936.

Ruelle, Ch.- E. *Collection des auteurs grecs relatifs à la musique.* Vol. 2, *Nicomaque de Gerase Manuel d' Harmonique.* Paris: Baur, 1881.

Sachs, C. *The History of Musical Instruments.* New York: W. W. Norton, 1943.

Seashore, C. E. *Psychology of Music.* New York: Dover, 1967.

Schlesinger, K. *The Greek Aulos.* London: Methuen, 1939. Reprint. Groningen: Bouma's Boekhuis, 1970.

Stanford, W. B. *The Sound of Greek: Studies in the Greek Theory and Practice of Euphony.* Berkeley: Sather Classical Lectures, no. 38, 1967.

Tarán, L. *Asclepius of Tralles: Commentary to Nicomachus' Introduction to Arithmetic.* The American Philosophical Society, vol. 59, part 4 (1969).

———. *Academica: Plato, Philip of Opus, and the Pseudo-Platonic Epinomis.* The American Philosophical Society, vol. 107 (1975).

Taylor, A. E. *A Commentary on Plato's Timaeus.* Oxford: Clarendon Press, 1928.

Thesleff, H. *An Introduction to the Pythagorean Writings of the Hellenistic Period.* Åbo: Åbo Akademi, 1961.

Waterfield, R. *The Theology of Arithmetic: On the Mystical, Mathematical and Cosmological Symbolism of the First Ten Numbers.* Grand Rapids: Phanes Press, 1988.

Winnington-Ingram, R. P. "The Spondeion Scale," *CQ* 22 (1928), 83-91.

———. *Mode in Ancient Greek Music.* Cambridge: Cambridge University Press, 1936.

———. "Ancient Greek Music 1932-1957," *Lustrum* 3 (1958), 6-57.

Index

Adrastus, 64, 65, 86, 95 n. 2, 105 n. 5, n. 7, 122 n. 15
Aelian, 131, 132, 138 n. 13
Alexandria, 14–15, 23
Amphion, 189
Antoninus Pius, 22
Aphrodite, 45, 47, 50, Fig. 1; 51, Fig. 2; 53, 56, 191
Apollonius of Tyana, 21–22
apotome, 135, 136, 185 n. 6
Apuleius, 14–15, 22
Archytas, 63, 121 n. 2, 130, 157
Ares, 45, 47, 50, Fig. 1; 51, Fig. 2, 53, 56, 191
Aristides Quintilianus, 71 n. 15, 96 n. 14, 139 n. 18, 158
Aristotle, 26, 28, 40, 43 n. 2, n. 3, n. 4; 58 n. 6, n. 7; 59 n. 10, 64, 65, 96 n. 14, 131, 139 n. 19
Aristoxenus, 21, 23, 40–42, 43 n. 5, 44 n. 6, 80 n. 9, 97 n. 17, 121 n. 3, 151 n. 8, 157, 170 n. 2, n. 4; 171 n. 13, n. 15; 178–81, 185–86 passim
arithmetic mean, 107, 116, 117, 118, 173
arithmetic proportion, 107, 181
arithmology, 18
Asclepius of Tralles, 24 n. 11
asyntheton, 133, 138 n. 17

Athenaeus, 18, 151 n. 8
aulos, auloi, 61, 67, 141, 147, 151
Aulus Gellius, 172 n. 23

Bacchius, 158
barbitos, barbiton, 74
Boethius, 15, 24 n. 8, 81 n. 11, 87, 95 n. 2, 139 n. 20, n. 22; 171 n. 13, 182, 186 n. 18
Bryennius, M., 80 n. 5, 81 n. 16, 158

Cadmus, 189
canon (kanon), 61, 65, 68, 71 n. 15, 88–89, 95, 96 n. 10, 144, 165
Censorinus, 86, 95 n. 2
Chalcidius, 86
chordotone (chordotonon), 85, 92
chromatic genus, 99, 155, 174
cithara, 61, 67
Cleonides, 158, 170 n. 4, 171 n. 3
comma, 135, 136, 185 n. 6
Commentary on Plato, 19
continuum, 39–41, 43 n. 3
Cratylus, 48, 58 n. 4
Ctesibus of Alexandria, 67

Damon and Phintias, 21
De anima, 65, 70 n. 5, n. 6

De caelo, 58 n. 6, n. 7; 59 n. 10
Demiurge, 107, 113–15, 122 n. 15
diabetes, 88, 96 n. 10
diatonic genus, 80 n. 2, 99, 138 n. 17, 155, 174
diazeuxis, 78
dieses, dieseis, 44 n. 9, 125, 131, 134, 135, 136, 139 n. 19, 171 n. 15, 175, 185
diezeugmenon (tetrachord), 110–11
Diogenes Laertius, 21, 96 n. 12, n. 14; 121 n. 4, 167, 172 n. 24
dioptra, 83, 89
dioxeian, 125, 130, 131, 132
Dorian nete, 75, 110
Dorian scale, 77, 88, 92, 100, 103, 105 n. 7
Doric dialect, 129–30
dynamis, 43 n. 2, 178, 185 n. 5

Earth, 47, 50, Fig. 1; 51, Fig. 2; 53
eide, 106 n. 8
ekbole, 44 n. 9
eklysis, 44 n. 9
energeia, 43 n. 2
enharmonic genus, 99, 155, 174
Epictetus, 22
Epigonus, 180
Epinomis, 60 n. 21
epochai, 47, 58 n. 2
Eratosthenes, 36 n. 8, 156, 165, 167, 172 n. 19, n. 20
ethos, 106 n. 10

Euclid, 14–16, 23, 25 n. 16, n. 17; 65, 66, 150 n. 6

Fabricius, 24 n. 5
fixed stars, sphere of, 52–54, 59 n. 16, 195
Fulgentius, 86

Galileo, 70 n. 10
Gaudentius, 86, 87, 95 n. 2, 96 n. 14, 158
genera, diagrammed: 184, Fig. 8
geometric progressions, 113–15, 117–18
Gerasa, 13, 24 n. 1
Glaukon, 96 n. 11, 97 n. 17, 185 n. 3
Glaukos of Rhegium, 93, 97 n. 17
gnomon, 97 n. 15
Greater Perfect System, 163, 164, Fig. 5; 171 n. 13

Hadrian, 34
harmonia, harmoniai, 19, 47, 57, 59 n. 8, 76, 77, 81 n. 14, 89, 100, 125, 129, 130–33, 135, 138 n. 9, 175
Harmonic Elements, 40, 44 n. 5, n. 6; 105 n. 5, n. 7; 121 n. 3, 170 n. 2, 171 n. 15, 185–86 *passim*
harmonic mean, 107, 116–18
harmonic proportion, 107
"Harmonious Blacksmith, The," 86
Harmony of the Spheres, 49–54
hendecachord, 162

henneachord, 69
heptachord, form of: 47;
   passim
Hermes, 13, 45, 50, Fig. 1; 51,
   Fig. 2; 53, 56, 80 n. 5, 189
Hermippus, 18, 25 n. 23
hestotes, 110, 121 n. 3, 174,
   183
Hippasus, 92–93, 123
Histiaeus, 160, 193
Homer, 101, 105 n. 3
Horace, 36 n. 1
hydraulic organ, 61, 67

Iamblichus, 15, 21, 26 n. 32, n.
   36; 58 n. 7, 86, 87, 95 n. 3, n.
   9; 105 n. 1, 137 n. 1
Idaean Daktyls, 87, 89
Immutable System, 158, 163,
   178, 183
Institutio Oratorio, 71 n. 14
interval (diastema), 63, 83,
   definition of: 61, 173, 177,
   180; distance on canon: 146;
   table of, 183, Fig. 7
Introduction to Arithmetic,
   15, 16, 17, 24 n. 10, 25 n. 15,
   105 n. 4, 121 n. 11, 122 n. 12,
   n. 13; 167
inverse proportion, 66–67,
   143–46, 147
Ion of Chios, 162
Isidore, Bishop of Seville, 14,
   86

Julia Domna, 23, 27 n. 42
Juvenal, 22

katapyknosis, 155, 164, 171 n.
   15, 178
Kepler, J., 52, 59 n. 9
kinoumenoi, 109, 174, 183
klepsiamb, 69
kollopes, 68
Kronos, 45, 47, 50, Fig. 1; 51,
   Fig. 2; 53, 55, 56, 191, 192

Lasus of Hermione, 97 n. 17,
   180
leimma, leimmata, 44 n. 9,
   115, 119, 123 n. 16, 127, 147,
   189–91
Lesser Perfect System, 171 n.
   14
Life of Apollonius of Tyana, 22,
   27 n. 42
Life of Pythagoras, 21
Linos, 74, 189
logos, 146
Lucian, 13, 24 n. 2
lutes, 68, 69, 100
Lycaon of Samos, 76, 81 n. 11
Lydian mode, 106 n. 11, 137 n.
   4
lyres, 61, 67–68, 73, 74, 80 n. 2,
   88, 100, 101, 131, 153, 171 n.
   11, 189

Macrobius, 86
magadis, 69
marriage number, 19–20
Martin, Th. M., 93, 97 n. 18
Mersenne, M., 66, 70 n. 10, 93
metaphor by analogy, 19–20, 26
   n. 28

Mixolydian mode, 75–76, 80 n. 9
modes, 71 n. 14
monochords, 61, 68, 71 n. 15, 96 n. 13, n. 14; 97 n. 20, 144, 145, Fig. 3
Moon (Selene), 45, 47, 50, Fig. 1; 51, Fig. 2; 52, 53, 55, 56, 191, 192
motion (kinesis), 49, 63–65
motion of the voice, 39–41
Mozart, W. A., 103–04
musical notes (phthongoi), 43 n. 1, names of: 45, 48–49, 153–55, 196; definition of: 61, 173, 177, 180; diagrammed: 175–76
Myth of Er, 52

Neopythagoreanism, 23
Newton, I., 97 n. 18
Nomoi, 197

octachord, 52, 59 n. 15, 75, 80 n. 2, 81 n. 16, 92, 100–01, 103, 105 n. 7, 143, 162
On Egyptian Festivals, 18, 25 n. 22
On Music, 16
On Nature, 125, 129, 130
On the Boring of Auloi, 151
Orpheus, 189

Pachymeres, G., 81 n. 16, 158, 160, 170 n. 6
pandoura, pandouros, 61, 68
Pausanias, 162

pektis, 69
pentachord, 102, 162, 171 n. 12, 193
Pherecrates, 161, 193
Philebus, 95 n. 10
Philo, 18
Philolaus, 23, 52, 59 n. 10, 121 n. 2, 125, 126, 128–36 passim; 139 n. 18, n. 19, n. 22; 147, 157, 167, 185 n. 6
Philostratus, 23, 27 n. 42
phorminx, 75
photinx, 61, 69
Physics, 43 n. 3, n. 4
plagiauloi, 61, 69
Plato, 18, 19, 23, 48, 52, 56, 60 n. 21, n. 22; 64, 65, 71 n. 14, 95 n. 10, 96 n. 14, 97 n. 17, 107, 109, 113–22 passim; 127, 128, 131, 135–36, 137 n. 3, n. 4; 156, 157, 161, 167, 168, 170 n. 1, n. 8; 172 n. 21, 185 n. 3, n. 6; 193, 194, 197
plectrum, 61, 69
Pliny the Elder, 76
Plutarch, 22, 114, 121 n. 5, n. 7
Pollux, 70 n. 13
Pompeia Plotina, 34
Porphyry, 14, 21, 26 n. 30, n. 31; 87, 95 n. 6, 138 n. 12, n. 13, n. 14
Proclus, 13
Prophrastus, 160, 193
psalterion, psalteries, 69
Ps.-Aristotle, 59 n. 15, 80 n. 6, 148, 151 n. 11
Ps.-Plutarch, 59 n. 15, 80 n. 7,

n. 8; 81 n. 13, 170 n. 7
Psychogonia, 107, 113, 121 n.
    5, 168, 195
Ptolemy, 18, 22, 25 n. 18, n. 20;
    26 n. 40, 95 n. 4, 97 n. 19,
    121 n. 2, 146, 157, 158, 170
    n. 3, 171 n. 14, 193
pyknon, 171 n. 15
Pythagoras, Pythagoreans,
    Pythagoreanism, *passim*

Quadrivium, 17
Quintilian, 68, 71 n. 14

Republic, 18, 20, 25 n. 24, 52,
    71 n. 14, 96 n. 11, 139 n. 21,
    170 n. 1, n. 8; 185 n. 3
regions of the voice, 37–38

St. Paul, 22, 27 n. 41
St. Peter, 27 n. 41
salpinx (trumpet), 61, 67
sambuka, 68
scale (*zugon*), 89
schema, schemata, 77, 80 n. 5,
    106 n. 8
schisma, 135, 136, 185 n. 6
Sectio Canonis, 65, 165
Septimius Severus, 27 n. 42
seven, the number, 56–57, 74,
    194
Simonides of Cos, 76
skindapse, 69
spadix, 61, 68, 70 n. 13
speaker hole, 148, 151 n. 9
species of the voice: continu-
    ous and intervallar, 37–38

spondeiasmos, 44 n. 9
stathme, 96 n. 10
Sun (Helios), 45, 47, 50, Fig. 1;
    51, Fig. 2; 52, 53, 55, 56, 191
syllaba, 125, 130, 131, 132
synaphe, 80 n. 5
syntheton, 138 n. 17
syrinx (panpipe), 61, 67, 100,
    149
systema, systemata, 47, 105 n.
    7, definition of: 173, 177, 181

Terpander, 53, 56, 59 n. 15, 74,
    75, 80 n. 4, 82, 189
Tetrabiblos, 25 n. 20
tetrachords, *passim*; form of:
    77; names of: 110, 153–55
Thamyris, 189
Theocritus, 71 n. 16
Theology of Arithmetic
    (*Theologoumena*
    Arithmeticae), 16, 24 n. 14,
    172 n. 26, 185 n. 7
Theon, 22, 26 n. 39, 60 n. 18,
    70 n. 3, n. 4; 97 n. 17, 122 n.
    15, 151 n. 10, 165
Theophrastus, 131
Thrasyllus, 22, 26 n. 39, 36 n.
    8, 138 n. 12, 156, 165, divi-
    sion of the canon: 166, Fig. 6;
    172 n. 18, n. 20
Tiberius, 22, 26 n. 39, 165
Timaeus, 41, 44 n. 8, 52, 56, 60
    n. 21, n. 22; 107, 109, 113,
    119, 121 n. 5, n. 8, n. 9; 127,
    135, 137 n. 3, n. 4; 139 n. 21,
    167, 168, 172 n. 21

Timaeus Locrus (Locrian
 Timaeus), 156, 167–68
Timon of Phlius, 167
Timotheos, 160, 161, 162, 171
 n. 11, 193
topos, 39–40, 43 n. 5
tornos, 96 n. 10

Trajan, 22, 34
triangular harp (*trigonon*), 61,
 68, 69

Zeus, 45, 47, 50, Fig. 1; 51, Fig.
 2; 53, 56, 191